KILL
THE BODY,
THE HEAD
WILL FALL

KILL THE BODY, THE HEAD WILL FALL

A CLOSER LOOK AT WOMEN, VIOLENCE, AND AGGRESSION

RENE DENFELD

WARNER BOOKS

A Time Warner Company

I have tried to present as accurately as possible my impressions
of the Grand Avenue Boxing Gym. I have modified
certain details about some of the individuals
in order to protect their anonymity.

Warner Books, Inc., 1271 Avenue of the Americas, New York, NY 10020
A Time Warner Company

Printed in the United States of America
First Printing: February 1997
10 9 8 7 6 5 4 3 2 1

Library of Congress Cataloging-in-Publication Data

Denfeld, Rene.
  Kill the body, the head will fall : a closer look at women,
violence, and aggression / Rene Denfeld.
      p.   cm.
  Includes bibliographical references.
  ISBN 0-446-51960-X
  1. Women—Psychology.   2. Aggressiveness (Psychology)
3. Violence.   I. Title.
HQ1206.D3651   1997
305.4—dc20   96-29127
                                                  CIP

Book design by Giorgetta B. McRee

For Jess

CONTENTS

CONTENTS

ACKNOWLEDGMENTS

There are people who help you out over the years, and they deserve repeated thanks. Thanks go to the Reddens—Jim, Joan, and Tony—and my family: Elaine Appleton, Dennis Denfeld, Charles Denfeld, Nichole Appleton, Michael Appleton, Eldredge Appleton, and my much-missed grandmother, Margaret Appleton.

My thanks also to Katherine Dunn for writing the foreword to this book. Katherine was one of the first writers to explore female aggression. She is a leading boxing reporter as well as novelist. I am honored by her contribution.

Doug Holm supplied valuable leads, while Bruce Anderson and Sparkle Fuller Anderson offered succinct boxing commentary. Promoter Mike "Motormouth" Morton was kind enough to answer my questions. There are many in the fight world here on the West Coast, including Steve Chase, Ray Monge, George Calderas, Richard Castro, Bob Jarvis, and Fred Ryan, whom I often watched, and listened to. I'm sorry their names didn't make it into the text.

My thanks to Bill Redden, who has always given freely of his time, and of himself.

ACKNOWLEDGMENTS

Most of all, I want to thank the trainers, fighters, and their families from the Grand Avenue boxing gym, past and present: Jess, Chuck, Ed, Fred, Mike, Bob, Isaiah, Miguel, Leon, Alberto, Javier, Lon, Tom, Billy, Anne, Johnna, Susan, Jose, Damion, Brad, Octavio, Isaac, Ron, Tim, and everyone else.

I hope they like this book.

FOREWORD

In November 1993, when Rene Denfeld first walked into the Grand Avenue boxing gym in Portland, Oregon, she had written and published widely on various social issues and, at the age of twenty-six, had just finished writing her first book (*The New Victorians*, Warner Books, 1995). But in the small, distilled world of the boxing gym, nobody knew or cared about her professional accomplishments. Her significance to the fight guys in that one small gym was strictly her gender. She was part of the first generation of women who were allowed to train and compete against one another as amateur boxers. For many of the men immersed in this sport, she was the advance edge of an invasion.

Women had been forbidden to box as amateurs until just the month before, October 1993, when U.S. Amateur Boxing, Inc., the national organization that governs amateur boxing, had finally been driven by discrimination lawsuits to open the sport to females. The fight guys were scared and their fears boiled down to two fundamental questions: Can women survive the game? Can the game survive women?

Similar dramas were being played out across the country as women and girls trickled into boxing gyms. But at the Grand, the focus was on Denfeld. As a longtime boxing reporter, I frequented that gym. As a woman and a supporter of women's right to participate, I anxiously watched her entry into the gym. She began with much the same attitude a twelve-year-old might have, intrigued by the sport and curious about her own capacities. She found herself under a microscope. Her demeanor as well as her ability and desire to respond to the rigorous training were analyzed and dissected by coaches, other boxers, and even this female reporter, as an example of what could be expected from all those women who would, in the ensuing years, infiltrate the ultimate male preserve—the territory of the warrior. It was an absurd and unfair burden to place on any individual, but there it was—inevitable.

Like most of the females who followed her into that particular gym, Denfeld was serious and eager. She was also a long-distance runner with enough stamina to impress the most relentless coaches. She didn't play coy or frail or ask that the game be changed to accommodate her. She asked to be allowed to play by the same rules as the boys. Given that chance, she proved her mettle. She changed a lot of guys' minds and earned their respect, not as a woman or a writer, but as something far more important in that context—a fighter.

That's how it looked from the outside, watching. But Denfeld's book reveals her deeper interior struggle. In the personal essays and sketches that introduce each chapter, she examines her experiences with fresh eyes and a lean, lucid narrative. Here she reveals her self-doubt, fear, frustration, delight, and wry humor. While she was being watched and tested, she was assessing the watchers, coming to understand their fears and the sources of their prejudices, and to sympathize even as she fought to overcome them. These sections of the book provide a point of view seldom revealed in the literary and journalistic treatment of the sport. This is the boxer's view. That this boxer is a woman adds complex new dimensions to an age-old experience.

Denfeld was not boxing so she could write this book, but the book was the logical result of her boxing. For Denfeld the writer, the ring becomes a lens to examine issues much larger than those surrounding one arcane sport. It exposes the cultural mythology surrounding women and aggression, and provides an opportunity to document the rich, multi-faceted reality that flatly contradicts the myths.

As Denfeld makes clear, the same superstitions and pre-conceptions that prevented women from boxing have traditionally excluded them from many other activities. And these beliefs are still commonly held in far more sophisticated circles by women and men alike. The crustiest of boxing's curmudgeons might well agree with some radical feminists and conservatives that women can be injured more easily than males, that they are dramatically weaker in physiological design and cannot develop strength. They would agree on the core belief that women do not possess the same aggressive capacity required for voluntary violence, that women are somehow further evolved, spiritually and morally superior to the crass inclinations to fight, more inclined to nurture and placate than to compete, and therefore more likely to be abused and exploited than to hold their own, to take care of themselves. Rene Denfeld says it isn't so, none of it. And she offers proof.

In 1960, just seven years before Denfeld was born, my high school physical education teacher gravely warned her female students that running too far or fast would render us permanently sterile. Believing her in those pre-Pill days of sketchy birth control, some of us took to pelting gleefully around the track at every opportunity. Now the women runners fly past my city windows at dawn, many of them mothers or future mothers, training for marathons.

Plenty of ignorance and fear, as well as outmoded tradition and misguided fantasy, are still tangled up in our thinking about human biology and behavior, and particularly about the limits of female ability. The last three decades have produced enormous progress toward legal and social equality for women in the United States. Still, at the brink of the twenty-first century, a major subtext for political and social debate is the physical and psychological difference between males and females. The presumption of significant differences between the sexes has traditionally affected our laws, social programs, educational systems, work opportunities, sports, and pastimes.

Denfeld explains that the old claims of difference have now boiled down to this most adamant core—the insistence that females are inherently less aggressive, less inclined to violence, than men. After introducing the reader to the gym and to amateur boxing through her own novice eyes, she considers the broadly defined concept of aggression and critiques the popular claims that females lack it. Armed with meticulous research, she discusses gender differences in terms of physical strength and the many social and environmental factors that influence them.

In subsequent chapters, Denfeld uses history, social and behavioral studies, and anecdotal evidence in seeking to understand the intended functions of the old mythologies and to reveal the reality that contradicts them. She considers the effects of an unnecessarily exaggerated fear of victimization on women's actual freedoms, and she debunks the popular notion that women rarely commit crimes. Her examination of domestic violence and child abuse is extensively documented, and it may be deeply disturbing to readers who have seen only limited media presentations of these crucial problems. Discussing the military, Denfeld reveals that modern circumstances make female participation mandatory, not just for civil rights but also for the practical good of the nation's armed forces. In chapter after chapter, Denfeld exposes some of our most central and cherished ideas of female nature as no longer functional.

The broad spectrum of aggressive behavior determines not just success but survival in every arena, from the boardroom to the barroom, from elected office to a night-darkened street. Denying that scope of behavior to an entire gender renders its members permanently dependent on the goodwill of the aggressors. Denfeld has maintained in all of her previous writings that protectionism is the primary cause of sexism. In this book, she demonstrates why such protectionism is neither desirable nor necessary.

This wider, more accurate definition of what it means to be female appears during a transitional period in our history. There is still resistance to females as full-fledged, multi-dimensional humans. The old strategy of sheltering women from the onerous burdens of real life and real risk are used not just by a male establishment but also by those who work for women's benefit.

But this political and academic rhetoric clashes dramatically with the growing dimensionality of women's lives. In fact, today's women are fighting fires, crimes, and wars. They are triumphing in the most intensive competition in business, science, political, and sports arenas. Rene Denfeld speaks from that reality in an often-personal but always-thoughtful confrontation with that mythology.

The joke is, of course, that fight guys, and fight reporters, are easy compared to the political dogma of women's mildness. Denfeld didn't have to explain to her boxing coach that women can be as aggressive as men. She just had to demonstrate. She won respect at the Grand even before she won in the 1995 Tacoma Golden Gloves. However entrenched and encrusted an individual's social notions, the fight folks are focused on their passion. When it comes right down to it, they will forget your race, religion, language, fashion sense, taste in music, and even gender, if you can fight.

—Katherine Dunn

KILL
THE BODY,
THE HEAD
WILL FALL

One ⟶

THE FIRST DAY
IN THE GYM

I first laid eyes on the Grand Avenue boxing gym while standing on the windblown street. I peered through the storefront window. The gym looked soft and musty, warm. Condensation ran in thick drops down the inside of the glass.

A series of peeling black plastic letters was stuck on the window. The letters read simply BOXING. On the weathered red door was a handwritten sign in English and in Spanish: "Members Only."

Nervously, I opened the door and stepped inside.

Here was a smallish room with faded wood floors.

A few fighters jumped rope or battered at bags. Some made a curious *huff, huff* noise as they threw their punches, expelling breath with each blow. Others made a strange whistling sound, like spitting with your tongue pressed against your teeth. This was a sound I would eventually adopt, to make the blows come faster, with that sting at the end, like a final syllable.

Old fight posters, scribbled with autographs, lined the room. A row of heavy bags dangled from chains. Long mirrors, smeared with fingerprints, leaned precariously against

1

one wall, next to a locker overflowing with gloves. A speed bag hung several feet above a wooden pallet, which was used to help children reach the leather punching bag.

A yellow line on the floor warned visitors to stay on one side of the gym. Old chairs were lined up so guests could watch the boxers work out. They were cracked and cheap-looking, salvaged from some defunct movie theater.

In one corner sat the gym's boxing ring, with soft elastic ropes and a stained canvas floor.

The ring looked huge, forbidding. Plastic buckets sat on the floor near each corner. During breaks, fighters swish water through their mouths and, leaning through the ropes, spit into these buckets. Sometimes this effluvia collects for days, with discarded tape and clots of expectorant blood floating in it, until the resulting liquid is black and foul.

The only sounds were the creaking of the bags and the soft whistling of boxers jumping rope. The place smelled like old sweat and leather: wet leather. There was something else, too, as ripe and healthy as cut fruit. It was the smell of fresh sweat when it comes in a downpour—the kind that is invigorating.

I fell in love right then.

As I made my way inside, gym bag in hand, the men stopped. They seemed in mild shock at a woman entering their world. A boxer with a pale Irish face quit jumping rope to watch me. He was dressed in a simple tank top and trunks, as poised and graceful as a gazelle, his chest rising and falling with his breath.

I was twenty-six at the time, small, almost petite. I looked nothing like a fighter.

I had come dressed to work out in old shorts and a T-shirt, having been forewarned there was no women's locker room. Feeling naked and ill at ease, I paused in the middle of the gym. A few older men turned. They were the trainers, old fighters with lean bodies and battered hands.

Boxing gyms are not health clubs or exercise gyms. Many exist on a shoestring budget, with barely enough equipment to function. You don't go there just to exercise. You go to learn how to fight. The dues include training. Every fighter, no matter how experienced, is supervised by a coach.

Within five minutes of my entering the Grand Avenue boxing gym, I found my coach: Jess Sandoval, an Hispanic ex-pro fighter in his seventies. Jess has steel-gray-and-black hair cut in crisp, close waves, a hatchet of a face, and hooded eyes. He was dressed in slacks and an open-collar short-sleeved shirt. Bent with arthritis and crippled with diabetes, he still looked dangerous and fierce. He didn't seem too thrilled about training a woman.

Stuttering shyly at me, Jess led me to a spot before the mirrors. Before he walked away, he told me to warm up. I stood there, stupefied and self-conscious. After a few minutes—with me doing some halfhearted stretches—Jess came back.

And he began what turned out to be a long, painstaking process: teaching a woman how to throw a punch.

Gently, over and over, he would form my fist correctly, show me the proper alignment of the shoulder, move my body to throw, show me the proper form. I didn't know the first thing about hitting. I would tuck my thumb inside my fist—a good place to get it broken. I would throw my hand out as if my arm were made of rubber, fall off balance, and promptly blush like a fool. I would stare at my feet as if they were small animals. I tried to move them in the precise, clean movements that Jess demonstrated—in the perfect balance that every fighter must learn—but what came out was an uncoordinated shuffling. I cringed as an old man next to me danced gracefully, his feet floating off the floor.

My first day in the gym passed in that haze of embarrassment we reserve for such difficult moments. I can barely remember it now. I know I pathetically tried to shadowbox before Jess finally told me I could stop and go home, sympathy on his face.

I look back now and think that it must have taken courage to go in there. But at the time, it was almost a lark. Bravado, not courage, carried me through.

The real courage would come later, when I actually stepped into the ring. It was then that I found out how terrified I was of conflict, the thought of being hit. And it was then that I discovered how gratifying it was to meet and grapple directly with my fear.

As the weeks and months passed, we made several false starts. Jess wasn't accustomed to training women. I think he felt that women had to be coached differently from men. Coddled, maybe. What does a boxing coach ask for from a female body? Is there a fundamental difference? He couldn't yell at me the way he would the men. I was a lady, after all. He didn't know what to do with me.

Everything you do in the boxing gym—everything—takes you one step closer to the ring. In shadowboxing, you watch yourself in the mirror. At the heavy bags, slugging at seventy pounds of dangling weight, you practice hitting hard as well as hitting with proper form. In front of the double-end bag (which the Mexican fighters call "the crazy bag," because the more you punch it, the harder it is to hit, and it drives you crazy), you duck and move and learn accuracy.

Lead with your left fist. This is the jab, used to pepper your opponent's face. You don't always hit hard with the jabbing left, but, rather, keep your opponent away, confuse him. The straight right hand is a power punch which I've only recently begun to grasp fully, having been too stiff before to throw my weight into it, hitting "like a girl." Arch the left arm and you have a left hook, which is a punch I'm much better at, using the leveled forearm to deliver the blow quickly, a series of them, as Jess softly chants, "Like a cat, like a cat."

The same hands that hit the face can hit the body. Except when you throw to the body—and Jess is an expert at body punches—you crouch, digging up from under, and use deep, hooking blows.

The straight line is strong and the wobbly line weak. The power of the punch is not in the muscle of the arm as much as in the weight and form of the body. Can you turn your hip into it? Move from the ball of the foot, collecting energy up the side of the body, and then send the punch sizzling out, with all the collected power snapping at the end of that tightly balled fist? It is more difficult than it sounds.

In boxing, you learn to use your body as a weapon. There is no ball, no bat, no lines on the floor, no goalpost or hoop. Most of the paraphernalia, the costumes, rituals, and excuses, of other sports have been trimmed away. What is left is exquisitely real, unavoidably frank.

At home, I ran more and more miles. In the gym, I worked harder and harder. I worked at the heavy bags until my arms felt puffy with exhaustion. I worked in front of the mirrors, on the double-end bag, on the speed bag. I worked until my shirt was soaked through, until the sweat ran down my legs, and I would go home as lathered as a hard-run horse. I worked until my face turned bright red (it still does, almost every workout). I worked until my shoulders took on the lean, spare look of a fighter—with each muscle clearly defined—and I noticed one day that the veins of my neck stood out, whether I was working out or not.

Pleased at my progress, Jess would wind the cloth wraps for protection around my hands and whisper boxing advice in my ear. His favorite was a famous adage, attributed most often to Muhammad Ali: Kill the body and the head will fall.

"You know what happens?" he asked me one day. Gesturing toward the in-curving line of my stomach, right under the rib cage, he said, "You hit them in the body. You do that, their legs don't work. They get tired and weak.

5

They are trying to make their legs move, but they can't. So they start thinking, I can't let her hit me in the belly anymore; I've got to stop her from hitting me there. And they drop their arms like this." Jess tucked in his elbows to protect his stomach, which made his fists drop slightly from his face, and looked at me with a question in his eyes.

I chimed in, "Their head is open. An unguarded target."

Jess nodded. His eyes took on a nostalgic, dreamy look, and, satisfied, he said, "The head will fall."

This is a society that condemns aggression in women. Boxing, of course, is one of the most aggressive of sports.

I didn't take up boxing to make a political statement. I had no intention of writing about it. I was looking for something different to do, a new hobby of sorts, something to get me out of the house and away from my work as a writer. Boxing seemed like fun, and it offered the bonus of physical fitness. I hoped it would convince me to quit smoking. Eventually, it did.

Who I am obviously informed my decision to take up the sport. I come from a background of taking risks (I left home when very young, for instance). While boxing did strike me as scary, it also felt like a challenge, and I love challenges.

But I soon found that boxing was not going to be a superficial endeavor. My experiences in the gym led me to question some of my most precious assumptions about aggression, and, in the process, about myself. A subject that had once seemed simple was increasingly revealed as full of shades and contradictions. It became harder simply to condemn all aggression. Such a perspective didn't seem to allow for the enormous differences between one kind of aggression and another, the purpose it serves, and what people get out of it.

For a word we use often, *aggression* is more of an umbrella term than one with a concise meaning. We use it to talk about a range of behaviors, from football to war. The dictionary will tell you that *aggression* means "a forceful action or procedure, especially when intended to dominate." That includes a lot of behaviors.

Aggression doesn't have to be physical. Trying to dominate and being forceful about it can occur in a Scrabble game. Nor does aggression have to be direct. Many people express force covertly, or hide it in groups. Witness the mobs that gather outside prisons during executions.

Nor is all aggression negative (the word *violence* is used to describe destructive, pointless aggression). A good deal of aggression, such as law enforcement, is considered positive—or at least necessary. It would be hard to dismiss the value of someone forcefully intervening to stop a crime. Sometimes taking action is unavoidable when defending ourselves and others.

We may cast it in polite language—such as *assertiveness*—but much aggression is an accepted part of our lives. We haggle in business dealings. We have countless ways to "make" children mind.

Everyone makes little determinations about what kinds of aggression are acceptable and what are not. For some people, boxing is repellent, but martial arts are wonderful. For others, television violence is detrimental, but spanking is key in raising law-abiding children. For still others, corporal punishment is immoral, but a woman who kills an abusive husband strikes a blow for womankind. It's hard to find a person who doesn't condone at least some form of aggression.

For all the behaviors that fall under the umbrella of *aggression*, however, there is one stereotype that defines it: It is considered male.

We now recognize that women can be just as smart as men, just as ambitious, and just as good at math and the sciences. But our views on aggression are still very old-fashioned.

Men are said to be more aggressive than women—more prone to violence and more interested in contact sports and other forms of direct action. Women are said to be more peaceful—less capable of violence and less interested in acting aggressively.

These differences are often cast as biological, starting from conception. Even when their premise is murky, many still consider this a major difference between the sexes—something that is deeply rooted, unalterable, a physical part of our landscape.

Women in fields such as law enforcement are gaining recognition. A few decades ago, there were only seven women police officers on regular duty in the entire United States. Now roughly one in ten officers and detectives nationwide is female. Women in such fields may not always be given the same respect as men, but at least there is an increasing awareness that they exist.

The same is not necessarily true for the negative side of women's aggression, especially when it pertains to crime, juvenile delinquency, racism, and other repugnant violence. The more overt and discomforting female violence, the more likely we are to deny it exists, especially as an important social issue with vast repercussions.

The result is that aggression is still viewed as "naturally" male. And female aggression is, by default, considered unnatural and uncommon.

The reality is this: Women can be just as aggressive as men.

Women get angry, become hateful, take out their frustrations on the helpless. In the 1920s, half a million or so women joined the Ku Klux Klan—nearly half the total Klan membership in some states.[1] American women supported the internment of Japanese-Americans in relocation centers, cheered on McCarthyism, and still continue to take part in a spectrum of violent crimes and extremist causes.

Oregon homemaker Shelley Shannon shot an abortion doctor and firebombed clinics. Self-styled revolutionary leader Linda Thompson fronts militia calls to overthrow the government.[2]

In Germany in 1991, women topped the list of most-wanted terrorists.[3] In Rwanda, women—including school-teachers—hatcheted and killed in a bloody civil war. Authorities say women played an overlooked role in that genocide, from nurses welcoming murder squads into hospitals to women wielding machetes in the massacres of entire families. One group of nuns supplied gasoline to burn Tutsis alive.[4]

Across the globe, women have shown themselves capable of the most grievous human faults, sins, and frailties of spirit.

Yet they have also shown themselves to be exemplary soldiers and athletes.

There *are* some general differences in how the sexes are socialized with regard to aggression. But these differences appear to be frequently exaggerated. To start with, relatively few men actually engage in violent behavior. Few want to partake in sports like boxing, and, despite popular images, even fewer are murderers or rapists. Aggression is held to be a defining aspect of masculinity, but this perception itself is frequently inaccurate.

At the same time, the public communication mill—from news coverage to the sciences—consistently disregards and downplays the myriad forms of female aggression. In all the press coverage of the genocide in Rwanda, for instance, few articles acknowledged that women took part. This erasure of women's violence occurs constantly, from family violence to terrorism.

The result is that women and men are portrayed as polar opposites in terms of aggression, when, in fact, we are more alike than we think.

The basic assumption that women aren't as aggressive as men is like the central leader on a tree: It forms the strong spine of a mythology. A surprising amount of popular thought traces back to this spine. On one branch might be found myths of female physical weakness. On another might be found lack of interest in female crime. A tangle of branches intertwine around notions of motherhood, and the denial of women's violence, especially within the home. The fruits of this mythology are numerous and litter many parts of our lives, from missed job opportunities to views on female sexuality.

In my mind, I see simple cutouts, shapes of women: Lizzie Borden, Ma Barker. Those few aggressive women history culls and passes down are unsatisfying and one-dimensional. If the history of women has truly been lost, as some claim, then part of this history is the obliterated record of female aggression.

I believe a great deal of social and personal confusion, if not harm, results from ignoring women's aggression. We ignore the tremendous pressures that can descend on anyone, the breaking point that leads to violence.

I know women who pride themselves on being nonaggressive but are ruthlessly competitive at work and unable to control their tempers. I've also known women who are dangerously violent, getting into fights when drunk, assaulting others.

But somehow, when women display it, aggression suddenly becomes a different issue. We change the language in the middle of the sentence.

Sometimes female violence is made light of. I think of the rock star Courtney Love, who has been accused of assaulting fans and fellow musicians. Love has gloated over her violence, and for the most part, the press has joined her self-romanticization. A male rock star who hit women would not receive this indulgent amusement, which Love doesn't seem to notice is patronizing: Fists in baby-doll dresses aren't taken as seriously as fists thrown by men.

Women's violence can be cast as a parody, with even the perpetrator invited to join in the joke. Laughter over the assaults of Courtney Love, or the more bitter-edged jokes about Lorena Bobbitt's slashing of her husband's penis, seem not just to discredit the act but to lessen the culpability of the person who commits it.

Women who enter once-male fields of aggression can be cast as oddities, even traitors to their sex. I have encountered the most sexism—the most outrageous displays of double standards and the most vicious personal attacks and vitriol—from other women. It is usually people who pride themselves on their lack of sexism who are the first to insinuate that I box, as one woman acquaintance said, "to get male attention." That would have to be the most painful and time-consuming method to do so ever invented.

Once, at a lunch table full of women writers, I was grilled by an author who was aghast that I boxed. Clearly discomfitted by the notion, she fell back on condescending pity, and then, casting about for a comforting excuse, she announced I surely suffer from high testosterone levels. This explanation was invented out of the blue and was completely unfounded, but the other women nodded sagely in agreement. I felt disheartened that boxing was such a radical departure from the norm that it could be explained only by a serious hormonal imbalance—something that would require medical treatment, something that could be "cured."

I am not saying that all women are by nature aggressive (neither are all men). What I am saying is that while violence is presented as the antithesis of womanhood, it is far more common than many think. It is not a humorous glitch or oddity, but a shifting, constant reality—the same as male aggression is. It is a human condition, not confined to one sex.

In activities like sports, women are being allowed to be more *publicly* aggressive.

These changes make a lot of people uncomfortable. I have friends who admonish me that "we should try to make men more like women, not vice versa." This thinking seems disingenuous to me. It bypasses the fact that inequality in public realms such as sports is at least partially the result of policy and discrimination. If women haven't been as openly aggressive, perhaps it's because we haven't been allowed to play. Such reasoning also denies the power that aggression has in society. A realm of power and influence—a culture, really—is denied to women but granted to men.

I'm not recommending boxing as a panacea for female inequality. That is not what this book is about. It is a lens on female aggression from the viewpoint of a boxing gym.

I also do not believe women should "embrace their dark side," as one writer put it, any more than men should embrace theirs. Such views glorify violence. I believe women's aggression is something that should be taken seriously. It is not cute.

But I do believe there are many women who, even if they would never step into the ring, dream of the power and freedom of physical confidence. They like to think that no matter what the situation might be, they will have the confidence to compete—to fight.

Many young girls fantasize about conflict: being a fearless leader of an army; leaving home to ride the trains, while fighting off sleazy hobos; being a detective and getting in fistfights with criminals. I remember long summer afternoons of my childhood spent stretched out on my bed, lost in vivid fantasies of being a gang leader, an Indian warrior. A good portion of these daydreams was spent in explaining the unbelievable to myself: How could I, a girl, be a gang leader? The complicated plots I would twist! I wanted desperately to be the protagonist of the adventure, but such protagonists came only in the male model.

Now I hear that the "new" breed of female detective novelists, such as Sara Paretsky and Sue Grafton, are starting to outsell the old romance novels of yesterday. I'm not surprised. There is a reason women love the books and movies that feed these fantasies, from the stories of Pippi Longstocking in grade school to the detective novels of Sue Grafton in midlife.

This is a time of upheaval. Women's place in society is changing, thus playing havoc with our beliefs about gender, while at the same time presenting new challenges. These stories validate the existence of aggression in women. They acknowledge that women grapple with this topic. In them, women dream of the day when they can fight; of a time when their fear will recede in the face of danger, until they are left with nothing but this sense of self: an awareness not just of their vulnerability but also of their strengths. Giving women a sense of indestructibility rooted not in naïveté but in a final recognition of their ability to survive—and win.

Two

THE SWEET SCIENCE

I started watching boxing because I had friends (women and men) who got together for big televised matches. We'd gossip and joke, and I barely paid any attention to the screen. If you had asked me, I would have said it was brutal and kind of ugly.

After a while, I found myself leaning forward to watch, increasingly avid and excited. I learned to differentiate the punches, so that fights were no longer simply a blur of fists, but, instead, a display of art—what has been called "the sweet science."

The term goes back to the seventeenth and eighteenth centuries, when young English gentlemen were trained in the manly arts of fencing, stick fighting, pistol shooting, and boxing. Boxing was, ironically, the least lethal of these forms of self-defense. Hence the name the "sweet" (meaning the safe) science.

I couldn't have taken up the sport myself if it hadn't been for a crucial court decision, won by a girl named Dallas Malloy only weeks before I entered the gym. Malloy was sixteen at the time, a muscular young woman with blond hair and wide-set blue eyes who sued to win the right for women to compete as amateur boxers.

In the United States, women had been fighting as professionals for some time, but amateur boxing—the respected, Olympic side of the sport—was off-limits until 1993.

Malloy made national news, angry that she wasn't allowed in the ring just because she was a *girl*. The judge agreed with her, so United States Amateur Boxing, Inc., which regulates all American amateur boxing, was forced to rescind its ban and allow women to compete against one another. Television cameras showed up for her debut bout, a historic first. Malloy won that fight, too.

A scant two years later, in 1995, almost five hundred women were registered as amateur boxers. For every woman registered to compete, there were probably a dozen training in the gyms. But that's still not many women, when spread across the country. Here in Oregon, I've never been able to compete in my hometown for lack of an opponent in my weight class (which is 116 pounds: bantamweight). I've traveled out of state for every bout.

The number of women registered as amateur fighters continues to rise. I hear snippets of information on the grapevine, details of women training in clubs, getting ready to compete. I suspect that within a few years a reasonably strong national women's amateur division will emerge. Most telling is that many women registering as fighters today are under age sixteen. They have the time and the energy to follow through, to make boxing part of their lives, and to make female boxing part of the sport.

Then the experience I lived through—my time at the Grand Avenue boxing gym—will be a fragment of history, the sliver of time when women first broke the barrier into this peculiar, and violent, sport.

* * * *

Boxing goes back to the ancient Greeks, but prizefighting grew popular in the late 1600s, with contests of bare knuckles and blood in the dirt of English village fairs.

Over a century ago, a series of refinements created the sport as we know it today, with ten seconds to get up from a knockdown and the right of the referee to stop a fight if the boxer can't defend himself.

Boxing has changed dramatically over the years. You can rent grainy films made the days before the neutral corner (after a fighter is knocked down, the referee today sends his opponent into a corner before giving the count). Fighters such as Jack Dempsey used to tower over the men they had just sent to the canvas, then club them as they tried to rise—like great lazy cats toying with their prey.

This is my sport, and I won't hide its sins.

Calls to outlaw boxing usually follow a fatality, such as the 1995 death of Jimmy Garcia, a superfeatherweight who fell into a coma after a technical knockout at the hands of Gabriel Ruelas. He died thirteen days later.

Garcia was tough and had what boxers call "a good chin"—he could take a punch. He had also dieted and dehydrated to lose thirty-two pounds in less than sixty days. According to some doctors, such massive dehydration might make fighters more susceptible to brain damage. The brain is suspended in a gentle well of water inside the skull, designed by nature to buffer blows to the head. Dehydration drains this fluid away.

Deaths in boxing are actually somewhat unusual. The incidence of brain damage is more common, although heavily debated. Some studies on professional fighters have confirmed cases of chronic neurological damage—the punch-drunk syndrome—while other studies on amateur fighters have not found any evidence of short- or long-term damage.[1] It seems arbitrary to me that one fighter who has fought only a handful of times will get injured, while others who fight hundreds of times remain lucid into old age.

It is not always the punch itself that causes harm, but the quick back-and-forth jarring of the head, causing the brain to slam against the interior of the skull. This is especially likely if the fighter is exhausted when he's punched and therefore his neck is relaxed and floppy, or if he falls and his head bounces off the canvas. A recent study on soccer players found they can receive similar injuries as a result of "heading" the ball.[2]

Headgear, which amateur boxers wear, absorbs much of this jarring effect. But headgear protects only the sides and top of the skull. It doesn't protect the nose, chin, or eyes, and it doesn't absorb the pain of getting punched.

Amateur boxing is considered a team sport. Coaches register their fighters under a team or club name. Larger cities are likely to have several teams. Even a small town will probably have at least one.

In the Grand Avenue boxing gym, there are two amateur teams. One is the Grand Avenue Boxing Club, headed by coach Ed Millberger, who has trained several national amateur champions, including the featherweight Andy Minsker. Ed is a stocky ex-fighter in his mid-seventies, with ears still lumpy with scars from the old days, before doctors discovered a simple technique to drain the fluid-filled cysts that can result from getting punched in the ears. In his time, the cysts would calcify and harden into bulbous scars, appropriately called "cauliflower ears."

The other team is managed by my trainer, Jess Sandoval, and is named after him: the Sandoval Boxing Club.

Amateur boxing runs contrary to all you have heard about boxing. The bouts are held in stark school gymnasiums or community centers, as dull a venue as that of a PTA meeting. The fans are usually polite and informed. When they yell encouragement, it is usually specific advice, such as "The right, Danny—he's open for the right," or "Work your jab."

It is advice yelled by people who know boxing, and as often as not if they think a fight is mismatched, or someone is getting hurt, they will yell that as well.

It may not pay, but amateur boxing has prestige—in an old-fashioned way. It's not unusual for celebrities or politicians, such as Arizona senator John McCain, to mention they once fought as amateurs. It connotes a certain respect, a sense of cleanliness and wholesome living, combined with a hardworking ethic and mental and physical hardiness.

Both amateur and professional boxing share some basic rules: no punching after the bell, no rabbit punching (hitting the back of the head), no blows below the belt and no kidney punches (the lower back), no holding and hitting.

You score points in amateur boxing regardless of the strength of the blow, but only for striking within the frame of the helmet and above the belt. But there is no scientific way to score boxing. Counting blows doesn't capture the art of the sport. "Ring generalship," or how classy, smart, and strategic one is in the ring, is important, and a challenger is expected to win clearly over a champion.

Amateur boxing is the training ground, in essence, for the Olympics, and then for professional boxing. Before women could fight as amateurs, the rare woman professional boxer would start her career as an adult with no competitive experience. The men, on the other hand, would often enter professional fighting with hundreds of amateur bouts on their record. Of course, the women in such a situation aren't going to be as good. It becomes a joke.

So allowing women to fight as amateurs—against one another in a women's division—has helped women's boxing as nothing else could. The days when women professional fighters had to don sexy outfits and crowds hooted in glee are gone. Now the women pros dress like the men (except they wear shirts, of course), train like the men, and can be quite gifted.

Once they see that women can have as much "heart" as men, some of the most adamant opponents of women boxing become enthusiastic fans. My fear that crowds would yell demeaning comments—sexual comments—never materialized.

It's something to see these men, old fight fans who can spend hours regaling you with stories of obscure past champions, who are honestly excited about women entering their world. It's easy to forget that commissions do not always speak for people, and that many men in this world may have missed sharing their passion with women.

There are still those who will never accept the idea of us "ladies" fighting. I have encountered men who are openly contemptuous of my efforts. For the most part, however, women fighters are quickly being accepted within the boxing world.

It is different outside it. When my face has been marked and bruised, neighbors and acquaintances grow uncomfortably silent, radiating sympathy. They think I'm a victim of domestic battery. If it were a man with bruises, they might think that he had gotten in a drunken bar fight, or had been smashed with a loose elbow during a basketball game. With a woman, they think victim, not aggressor.

The techniques of boxing may run counter to human instincts (which in a confrontation are to kick, hit out wildly, cringe, or run in big batty circles), but the core ability is always there, and anyone can learn.

There is no special killer instinct that only boxers possess, but something so innate to all of us that it takes only training, and the decision to compete. It is a switch that can be turned on so easily, it takes just that one split second: Bell rings; it's time to fight.

The violence of the boxer is not the violence of a mugger or rapist. It is not the violence of people filled with rage or driven to hurt. Many inexperienced with boxing see a fight as a flurry of emotion, a sport of bloody conquest. But emotion is the enemy of boxing, and it is discouraged. The fights themselves are calculated, impersonal. The punches are timed.

The aim of the sport may be to pummel your opponent, but this goal exists in an odd state without anger and, in most cases, without dislike. Your mind is there, disembodied. You are thinking, planning, maybe even admiring your opponent while you work.

There have been times I have felt closer to a sparring partner than to just about anybody else, with feelings of genuine intimacy passing between us, even as we snap blows. In a sense, you are sharing a profound respect. You agree to hit each other, as equals, on an equal level, in this safe place, with no hard feelings.

In the lore of boxing—which is sometimes accurate—a fighter who seriously injures or kills his opponent becomes racked by guilt, unable to fight again, his heart taken out of him. When Gabriel Ruelas put Jimmy Garcia into a coma, he was desolate. For days, he kept a vigil by Garcia's hospital bed, studying his swollen lips and head. "I pray for Jimmy," he said, "and I pray for myself."[3] The next day, Garcia died.

Unlike the mugger or rapist, the boxer usually doesn't want to hurt his opponent—their face, perhaps, but not their sense of self, not the part of people damaged through assault, that indefinable place of true vulnerability. Rape and other assaults are defined by the terror of the victim. Their core safety is violated. It is a different thing to act in a sport such as boxing, where both parties understand the rules and where the aggression is mutual.

Curiously, the rules of the sport prevent a personal attack. No matter how one might try, he or she cannot cross certain lines into destructive, personal violence—one cannot take off the gloves, strike outside the prescribed lines, attack in a way that fundamentally humiliates. The difference in context may seem slight, but in action it is profound.

It is an entirely different thing, a world apart.

More than anything, going into the gym has led me to question: What causes aggression? Is it true that women tend to be less aggressive than men? Are women never interested in dominating others? If so, why not? Is it evolution? Animal instinct? Hormones?

Or given the same sport and the same training as men, would women show themselves to be similar people?

From the shape and strength of our bodies to the ability to act decisively, I believe aggression is less a stronghold of biology than a house of cards being tumbled aside, a thin line transgressed with one firm step into the ring.

Three ✦

ARE WOMEN THE WEAKER SEX?

The first time I got into the ring to spar, I was so nervous, my knees were shaking. Jess fitted the damp, smelly leather helmet neatly over my head and ears, leaving my face exposed. He laced the fourteen-ounce training gloves on next. They felt like foreign growths on my hands, heavy and bulky, and I flexed my fingers inside their sweaty interiors, feeling the empty spaces.

With the gloves on, I was helpless as a baby. I couldn't blow my nose, wipe the sweat out of my eyes, or do anything else requiring fingers. Jess popped my mouthpiece in with quick fingers that tasted, briefly, of salt.

I set my face into composed lines, shuffled my feet, and tried not to let anyone know just how scared I really was. The men gathered around. They watched, mouths ajar at the novelty of a woman entering the ring, until the coaches began bellowing, "Get back to work."

The eighteen-year-old Hispanic man who had been picked as my sparring partner—because of his weight of 118 pounds—was already in the ring, shadowboxing to loosen up. The bright lights of the gym glinted off his muscled arms and narrow shoulders. He was dressed in high-top orange shoes, a light tank top, and soft cotton trunks. The heavy leather belt (for crotch protection) fitted snugly over his trunks, cupping his groin. Under the shadow of his helmet, his face—with heavy lips and brown eyes—looked blank in concentration. I learned later that his name was Octavio.

There was only one thought in my mind: I am going to get hit.

The idea frightened me more than I had imagined. Once I realized—at gut level—that getting punched was unavoidable, I ran into twenty-six years of social indoctrination like a brick wall. I was afraid I would freeze. I was afraid it would hurt. I had visions of women being hit in the movies: cringing, helpless, pleading.

Jess gave me a careful, considering look. Then he pointed his head toward the ring.

I climbed through the ropes and stood on the gritty, unfamiliar canvas. I raised my fists. The gloves, padded, loomed like red balloons in front of me. For a second, I couldn't remember if I had my fists turned properly. I couldn't remember anything. My mind went blank; my few months of training vanished. I took a deep breath. Okay, here goes, I thought.

The bell rang. My sparring partner looked up at me from under his helmet, bit his lips, and crossed himself. He shifted forward slightly, his legs moving under the long trunks. I forced myself forward, uncertain, my feet numb and clumsy.

My training returned: I threw out a few jabs.

Nervous, he responded: a stinging jab to my nose. I lunged at him, overexcited, trying to hit him with my jab, throwing wild rights. He slapped me politely on the ribs, landed a few more jabs.

And I thought, That doesn't hurt so bad.

Somehow, that realization was more exciting and fulfilling then I could ever have imagined. I was being hit by a man. But I wasn't falling to pieces. I was going to be okay.

I hit him back as well as I could, lacking his skill yet having just as much perseverance. Bobbing and weaving across the ring, breathing raspily through our mouthpieces, we flicked jabs, rights, and body blows. I was going too fast, getting too wound up. Jess made a soothing sound from the side of the ring.

We kept eye contact the entire time. Even in the heat of battle—how curious, that tempestuous term for what turns out to be so quiet, almost peaceful—I noticed little things: his eyelashes, the shadow by the cusp of his nose. A bubble of mucus appeared under his left nostril. We were both prickly with heat, and breathing raggedly. Our faces were scant inches apart, close enough to kiss.

Thwack. I saw that coming, the right, and still walked directly into it. When you get smacked in the nose like that, it is quick, stunning—painless in an odd way, and yet disturbing: a thick, diffuse, blotting sensation. Desperate, I plowed into him, and he captured my arms in a quick clinch, turned me deftly against the ropes, and spun me out again. Jess made a snorting, derisive noise from the side of the ring. I barely had time to feel like a fool (I learned how to store these moments for later self-castigation) before we were hitting each other again.

Time held still, counted only by blows: a jaw-rattling left hook to my chin, a surprisingly stunning straight right, a jabbing left peppering my face. Later, I became aware how much he was babying me—how light the punches actually were. At the time, they seemed more than enough. Boxers call it "glove-shy": the sense of shock at being hit, not because of pain, but more from the invasion of privacy, the body shock of it. You close your eyes and wince involuntarily.

Only through sparring do you eventually lose your glove shyness, learn how to look straight into your partner's eyes, and cease to blink when hit.

I became aware of a stitch under my ribs, sweat trickling under my helmet, my nose running. I could hear all the sounds of the gym—Jess giving calm advice from the side of the ring, someone hitting the heavy bag, guys conversing in quiet tones, the ten-seconds-to-go buzzer—yet at the same time it seemed that the world had narrowed down to just us, two bodies pitted against each other. I got through with a strong right hook to his rib cage and felt a rush of hot pleasure to see his eyes blink in startled pain.

When the bell rang, we stopped immediately. We didn't grin at each other and slap our gloves together. That would come later. But we did smile shyly at each other. And I walked out of that ring feeling as if I were floating. I had done it.

My face was tender, and later it bruised slightly. I lay on the couch that evening, seraphic with exhaustion, nearly bursting with pride.

My brother tells me that women shouldn't be allowed to compete physically against men, because men are stronger.

I think of my brother's words and I think about sparring with Octavio, and the countless times I have sparred with men since. Whom else am I going to spar against, without any other women in the gym who compete?

Octavio was more than my first sparring partner. He was a revelation. I had never competed physically with a man before, and certainly not on such intimate—and equal— terms. His arms, his legs, the shape of his torso—they were nearly the same as mine. We had more in common than not, outside of his cup, my chest guard, my wider hips, and his longer legs. He was far more skilled than I, but mostly because he'd been training longer.

At that time, most of the men at the gym were much better than I. They could hold me off with their fists, show off. Questions of superiority were moot. The playing field wasn't equal, and there was no pretense it should be. Beginning fighters always start with more experienced fighters, because putting two green boxers in the ring is just asking for an out-of-control punching match. A more experienced fighter can teach without hurting a newer fighter or getting hurt himself.

Now sometimes I'm the more experienced fighter climbing through the ropes. I discover the feeling that Octavio must have felt with me: how careful experience can make you. Usually the fighter is male, and so the status has been reversed. These newer fighters cannot hide behind chivalry. There have been times when I've gone into the ring with men who were almost incapacitated by the fear they would get beaten, and embarrassed, by a girl. Each time in the ring can be a struggle.

When I suggest to my brother that maybe some women are just as strong as some men—or that maybe strength difference doesn't matter as much as skill—he responds with derision. Men shouldn't compete against women like that, he says, because it is unfair.

Men, he says, are just stronger.

Maybe men are not stronger—or at least not always, and not in the ways we assume.

I, too, had always thought that by nature men are stronger than women. I assumed that they must have some magical property to their muscles, some innate difference in fiber, structure, or size that makes a bicep that looks just as stringy as mine burst with male virility.

It came as a surprise to learn that this isn't the case. Strength differences between the sexes are not that profound, nor are they set in stone.

27

Generally, women are about two-thirds as strong as men. This is partially due to men's greater size (they have more muscle mass). When researchers compare men and women of the same height and weight, they find differences substantially decline.[1]

Many such differences in strength are based on activity. The same studies that show men are stronger also indicate that this disparity is concentrated in the upper body, less so for the lower body.[2] This is because both sexes use their leg muscles in daily walking and in exercises such as jogging, while men are far more likely to engage in exercises such as weight lifting or to work in jobs that involve digging, carrying, or heavy lifting—activities that target their arms and shoulders.

In January of 1996, the U.S. Army released a study confirming that women are capable of performing all the military tasks once reserved for men, providing they are given the training. The army discovered that women can easily increase upper-body strength to meet the most demanding physical requirements, including running a two-mile course through the woods while carrying a seventy-five-pound backpack.[3]

The women in the army study were not weight lifters or brawny marines. They were civilian students and others who had volunteered for a strength-training course. Many had never exercised before. Several were mothers who had recently given birth.

I wonder how much female strength is affected by our conviction that we can't—can't open the pickle jar, turn the compost, dig a ditch, or throw a ball. I still find myself mutely handing the splitting maul over to my boyfriend, assuming he can split more firewood. And he can, from a lifetime of practice.

In one thought-provoking experiment done some years ago, subjects were tested for strength after being exposed to suggestions of weakness or power. Following the suggestions of weakness, strength scores plummeted. Suggestions of greater strength increased the subjects' results. The authors concluded that psychological factors may play an important role in physical ability, which leads to the interesting question of how much women's strength is affected by constant reminders of weakness.[4]

In my experience, it does seem men my size are slightly stronger. I don't know if this is the result of a lifetime of physical activity, biological differences, individual differences, training, or a combination of all these factors.

When I find myself thinking that men are hopelessly stronger, however, I remember my first real boxing match, against a woman who can punch harder than most men. And I think of some of the men at the gym who are decidedly weaker than I am.

The idea that women aren't as strong as men still has remarkable impact on our lives. Whether women feel safe walking to their car at night; whether men treat us patronizingly when we tackle physical tasks; whether women are welcome in jobs such as construction; whether girls are invited to join in when boys play—our lives are still defined by assumptions about our bodies.

Intrinsic to our understanding of what our bodies are capable of is what we think drives them. We have the notion that aggression is innately a male characteristic and not a female one: A ferocity that is the birthright for one sex—and unavailable to the other.

Once a trainer was telling me I had to *get more vicious,* and Jess interrupted him, shaking his head: "She isn't like that," he said under his breath.

Meaning, I'm a woman: a feminine-looking woman with long hair and polite manners. Until recently, Jess had trouble recognizing that a woman could have that same core of aggression a man can have. He clearly believed that I am too sweet, too kind—too feminine and female—to be mean.

Later, Jess seemed to revise his views. I don't think he was motivated by any intellectual exercise, but, rather, by seeing other women fight, and, perversely, by a feeling of protection: He didn't want me to get hurt. The axiom always rings true: The best defense is a good offense.

I think Jess also began to forget that I'm female. He started treating me as a fighter. Sometimes he would reach out, reflexively, to pat me on the behind, only to find his hand frozen inches away from my tush.

It's a scene, we are told, as old as mankind. A hulking caveman is standing near a fire. In one hand, he holds a club; in the other, a carcass of some sort. In front of the fire is a cavewoman—cooking, of course. In her hands are not the instruments of the hunt, but those of domesticity. At any moment, he might drag her off by her hair.

The idea that men are biologically predestined to be more aggressive than women—the evolutionary result of a prehistoric past, genetically imprinted on the mind—has ongoing popularity, a theme played in endless reruns by popular culture.

It's an argument appealing for its simplicity, but on close appraisal, it's more like an old sweater full of little holes. Despite all the work of scientists to find the "criminal gene" and other efforts to name a biological reason for human aggression, none has ever been found.

The hormone testosterone, for instance, has proved impervious to efforts to prove it causes aggression. Researchers have found both sexes manufacture considerable quantities of the misnamed "male" and "female" hormones (the male body, for instance, is reliant upon estrogen for bone growth). The complex nature of these hormones makes it difficult to prove which is having what effect. Recent studies have suggested that if there is a hormonal influence to aggression, it may be *estrogen*. Adolescent girls given estrogen treatments for delayed puberty showed increased aggression; so do male mice given the hormone.[5]

We are still far away from understanding precisely what role—if any—biology plays in behavior. Correlations have been found between high lead levels and extreme violence in children.[6] Some disorders, such as schizophrenia, are also associated with the increased likelihood of violence, though most schizophrenics are nonviolent.

Yet the countless social factors to be considered—gun availability, absent parenting, schools, values—seem to offer more possibilities than purely biological explanations. Even in instances where physical factors may play a role, environment would appear to dictate the outcome. A schizophrenic individual who is given the proper medication and family support is going to behave differently from one who is deinstitutionalized and left homeless.

No single factor can explain aggression. When confronted with another bit of evidence shaking his theory, an author who claims that single parenting causes crime once complained that he was "getting that complexity feeling." To me, "that complexity feeling" seems unavoidable when discussing aggression.

Unfortunately, many writers seem anxious to avoid any complexity feeling, skating thinly over conflicting evidence in an effort to prove predestined differences between the sexes. To give just one example, in his book *The Red Queen: Sex and the Evolution of Human Nature*, writer Matt Ridley uses the statistic that 93 percent of drunken drivers in the United States are men as proof that male aggression cannot be explained by "social conditioning alone."

But in the decade between the publication of this statistic (1983) and the publication of Ridley's book (1993), the percentage of American women arrested for drunk driving nearly doubled.[7] For me, this hints that gender differences with regard to drunk driving *are* due to social conditioning. The rising rates represent not evolutionary change but a simple increase in the number of women driving. As women drive more, the percentage who do so drunk will continue to rise.[8]

The dismaying thing about biological approaches to aggression is that instead of exploring the topic of aggression, they focus on explaining it—quickly, and politically. That's the beauty of biopolitics: If you say something enough times, it becomes a matter of common sense. If you maintain that men are more aggressive, you cut all the evidence to the contrary off at the knees. Who wants to talk about women who drive when drunk? They simply don't do it.

I believe people have a *potential* for aggression—which is different from a *drive*. Aggression is like language. An infant can learn it, but it does not come programmed and pre-taught (the nature of behavior always involves an element of invention). It is not inevitable or necessary that any of us act aggressively.

But while we are not driven to aggress, we all have the ability to do so. Each aggressive behavior is a potential that, depending on the situation, is nourished, dissuaded, or ignored by our communities and our families—sometimes directly, sometimes inadvertently.

Some of the fighters bring their children and wives to wait while they work out. There is one beautiful little girl with coffee-colored skin and eyelashes as fine as embroidery who boasts her own set of tiny boxing gloves. Dressed in a pinafore, church shoes, and boxing gloves, she followed me one day as I warmed up by throwing punches, mimicking my every move.

I have a friend who tells me about another girl, her oldest daughter. The girl is obsessed with dresses and playing princess games. She won't leave the house unless she is dolled up to the nines. Her mother has bought her plenty of pants and rough-and-tumble toys, but the daughter isn't interested. Now the mother wonders if gender differences with respect to aggression are innate after all. Why else would her daughter end up wanting to dress like a princess every day?

Rather than being biologically determined, behavior may signify other socialization the child receives—from grandparents, neighbors, teachers—as well as subtleties in our own parenting that we aren't aware of. While parents may give their girls trucks to play with, not very many allow their little boys to dress up as fairy princesses and encourage them to put on mom's perfume. I believe biological assumptions allow us to avoid addressing the many ways we still treat boys and girls differently.

Some of us do learn to be nonaggressive when we are young. But early training can be rejected later, forgotten in moments of anger, decisively conquered, or dismissed behind closed doors. In a famous 1963 Yale experiment in which college students were allowed to administer electric shocks to a victim, women showed themselves just as likely to aggress as men. In fact, the female students were more inclined to push the high-voltage button, and to keep their finger pressed on it, even as their victims gave tremendous cries of pain and distress.[9]

Who knows where people's lives will lead? The potential for aggression remains, and the girl who plays fairy princess at age six may end up a rugby coach, a tough criminal lawyer, or even in prison.

Or she may end up like that little girl looking up at me as she secretly followed my steps, her black shoes clickity-clatting across the floor, a warm draft of air pillowing the

33

yellow dress above her brown legs. Laughing, her father commented, "Now that's what I call shadowboxing."

One day, a young fighter came up to me, excitement in his eyes. He was maybe eighteen, with a tattooed, wiry frame and bristle-cut hair.

"Jess says I get to spar next week," he announced. I congratulated him. He added, "Jess said it was with a female, so I guess it's with you. I don't see any other females in here fighting."

I never react anymore, hearing myself referred to as "female," a strangely clinical word. I know no one means any ill by it. The men at the gym use it sometimes instead of a word like *woman* because it is more neutral. A *woman* is someone you may see romantically, but a *female* is just another aspect to a person, like her weight class. I appreciate the intent behind the word choice, the effort to place my gender aside, to make me into another fighter, who happens to be female.

I tried to make him feel at ease, mentioning I needed to work on my defense (unstated meaning: I won't hit you much). He nodded, agreeing. "You'll work on your defense, me on my offense, right?"

Then, eyeing my blocky shoulders, he added with sincerity and worry, "You'll take it easy on me, won't you?"

Not too long ago, I was asked if I believe women should be able to compete against men in the ring—for real, for titles. My response was immediate. Of course. Not just because women in boxing are marginalized by lack of competition but also because I believe that women can do it.

Maybe not this year, or even this decade, but someday, with the proper training from an early age, a woman could attain the skills needed to compete against men on the professional level—especially at the lower weight classes.

The person who asked me (it happened on an English radio station, actually) seemed shocked at my answer, and he promptly began to bluster. What, he wanted to know, if women get hurt?

"Not us," I responded. "Them."

Perhaps that is the fear underlying so many of our beliefs in strength differences, in innate versus learned aggression, in the fair sex versus the strong. It's the fear that, given an opportunity, a woman matched against a man just might, as horrible as it sounds, beat the dickens out of him—that we will not take it so easy on men after all.

That kid never did come back in the gym to spar.

Four

WOMEN IN ANGER: THE STEREOTYPES PROVE FALSE

I always say," Chuck Lincoln told me as we climbed through the ropes, "that anger has no place in the ring. You are here to work." Chuck is a coach who sometimes helps Jess with my training. A lean black man of about sixty, he has a creased face and short, grizzled hair. He dresses in neatly pressed casual clothes.

Chuck, at that moment, seemed pretty angry himself, in his derisive way. As I had been getting ready to spar, two of the fighters got into an unsporting altercation. One was an older ex-professional with methodical movements, a stocky black man named Ron. Past his prime, Ron is still a good sparring partner, willing to mold his style to help someone else.

He was sparring with a myopic-looking white kid, maybe eighteen years old, who had a nasty shiner over one eye. The kid is known for not being able—or willing—to pull his punches. When he spars, he gets in there and brawls, and the other fighters seem to disrespect him for it.

The trouble began halfway into their second round. The younger man was throwing his punches far too hard for sparring. He was windmilling, acting crazy. Ron, the ex-pro, seemed baffled by this at first, ducking neatly out of the way and muttering for the guy to cool it.

The kid threw a roundhouse right, with all his shoulder into it. The blow was hard enough to drive the sweat out of Ron's hair, sending a spray across the ring.

With a disgusted look, Ron promptly spat his mouthpiece on the canvas. He asked, baffled, "Now why do you want to go and act like that?"

But the kid belted him again, though Ron's arms were down and relaxed, and the sparring session obviously over. The blow hit Ron neatly in the side of the face, and he simply stood there, a look of complete disgust on his face. Then the kid belted him again, silently, and again, a series of rights. "That's how I work," the kid said, and smashed Ron yet again. Still, Ron didn't raise his gloves. Finally, he said, out of the side of a bruised mouth, "That ain't work. You don't know what the hell you're doing. You aren't a boxer. You don't know what it means. You want to fight? Fine, let's take off these gloves and go outside."

It was at this point—with the altercation quickly moving toward a brawl—that Chuck stepped in. "Cut that crap," he commanded, and the kid stormed out of the ring. Ron apologized for the ruckus, then climbed out himself.

It turned out that the kid had lost his most recent fight just a few days before. I heard that he lost because of his temper. He gets angry and blows it. Goes in throwing great granny shots, out of control, and leaves himself wide open—walks right into his opponent's blows and gets beaten.

Anger, Chuck admonished me again, will make you lose. You get tired, and stupid. Boxing isn't about getting mad, he said. The contempt in his voice for anyone who would think so stayed with me as my sparring partner climbed onto the canvas behind me and touched my glove briefly before the starting bell rang.

* * * *

Ask a group of women about anger and you will probably hear an intake of breath, a moment of consideration—and then you'll get an earful. For many women, anger is a subject fraught with fears, guilt, and embarrassment. Men get angry, too, and feel guilty for it. But women confront a frustrating mixture of pop psychology and denial that men usually don't.

On one hand, we acknowledge that women get mad. There is a folklore built around angry wives with rolling pins and upset moms brandishing hairbrushes. Nearly everyone remembers a time when their mother, sister, or wife just about lost it, or did lose it. They might have screamed out their frustration, criticized, stormed, yelled, spanked, slapped. We all remember angry women.

On the other hand, women's anger is still viewed differently from men's. The causes, from whining children to messy husbands, are seen as trivial. The anger itself is thought of differently—less embodied with physical threat and potential harm, less dangerous to society, less important in general. If women get mad at their husbands, it is not viewed in the same way as husbands getting mad at their wives. Male anger contains a threat. Female anger, if it contains anything, is deemed bitchiness or laughed off as a joke.

Lately, several of my friends have become mothers. All tell of the shock they felt the first time they flew into a rage at one of their children. "I wanted to *kill* her," one friend said of her colicky baby, who had kept her up for nights, crying incessantly. Many new mothers will say how amazed they are at this murderous anger surfacing, and how alone—and how guilty—they feel in dealing with it.

There is not much public recognition of the physical danger a woman can pose to a baby. Told her entire life that her anger is minor and her aggression inconsequential, a woman may be blindsided by her ability to hurt another. The result, as one of my friends says, is the feeling "that there is something wrong with you."

Conventional wisdom has it that there are dramatic differences between the sexes in terms of anger. In her best-seller *The Dance of Anger*, psychologist Harriet Goldhor Lerner claims that women "have long been discouraged from the awareness and forthright expression of anger. Sugar and spice are the ingredients from which we are made."

The classic stereotype is that women play sweet when angry, stifle their emotions, and then lash out in backstabbing or are consumed with shame. Lerner calls this the "Nice Lady Syndrome."

But author Carol Tavris, in her book *Anger: The Misunderstood Emotion*, explains how research shows exactly the opposite. There are actually few differences between male and female anger. According to Tavris, "of the many studies that have surveyed the kinds and causes of anger, very, very few have uncovered any sex differences. . . ."

In one study Tavris cites, men and women were asked to describe an experience they had had with anger during the previous week. The study found both sexes get angry at the same people (loved ones head the list; second is someone known and disliked). The majority responded verbally. A substantial minority (12.5 percent) of both sexes became violent—slapping, hitting, or throwing objects.

Women in this study were just as likely as men to become physically aggressive when angry. Men were just as likely to fit the "feminine" mode of coping with anger, such as trying to talk about the incident.

Such studies show that gender is not an indication of how someone will react to anger. It seems to be more an individual matter. Some women yell, scream, and hit. Some men get quiet. Then why the continuing belief that women suffer from such things as the Nice Lady Syndrome?

Tavris examines another study by anger specialist Don Fitz; it offers one explanation. Like other researchers, he found few differences between adult men and women. But there was one important exception. Men are more willing to get visibly angry in public—at rude cabdrivers, for example—while women tend to get openly angry only in private.

That women confine displays of anger to the home, while men get angry in public, may help explain why we believe women get angry less often than men.

But there is also, I feel, the value attached to anger. Part of the reason we think women are unable to express anger is that we interpret it differently when it occurs. A woman snapping angrily at her husband in a bookstore might receive a raised eyebrow or two, but a man speaking angrily to his wife in the same tone will set off emotional alarms. Everyone will bristle.

Later, we might remember the man and his anger, and perhaps worry over his wife. The angry woman recedes to the back of our minds.

We fear male anger will lead to violence. Women's anger just doesn't count.

Women frequently hear we need to express our anger more. We are told to "let it out," "communicate our feelings," and "blow off steam."

I've had several people comment that boxing must be a great way to release anger. At first, I thought that might turn out to be true. But after boxing for a time, I began to think that hitting the bags—or another person—was not causing any appreciable decline in my level of anger.

If anything, boxing seemed to make my anger a little worse. I don't know if this was due to stress unrelated to the gym or because boxing was validating using my body aggressively, which was bound to have an impact on my anger.

There is a negative psychological aspect to being physically empowered: It is the mark of every bully.

And so I found myself feeling not a cathartic drain of anger but instead a dangerous awareness of my ability to aggress. Rather than drain away frustrations, going into the gym simply made me more likely to conceive of expressing anger physically. Of course, exercise is a good release of tension. Anytime you use your body vigorously, you will feel good. But for me, exercise doesn't tackle the causes of anger, and therefore can't reduce it.

I believe the popularity of the catharsis approach, where women are told they need to release their anger (while men are told they need to keep theirs in check), is an indication of how lightly female anger is taken. When therapists and writers tell women to stop stifling anger and let it go, they rarely seem concerned with the effects this release may have on children, family members, and others.

Some writers appear to believe that just about every problem a woman can have is rooted in "toxic" suppressed anger. In their book *Female Rage*, authors Mary Valentis and Anne Devane claim "unacknowledged female rage" expresses itself in phobias, panic attacks, manipulation, passive-aggressive behavior, chronic fatigue, suicide threats, headaches, eating disorders, and a multiplicity of other symptoms.

Evidence doesn't support these sorts of claims. Anger is not a physical property in the body, like an infection or a cancer, that must be discharged or removed. If suppressed, it will not migrate to the stomach and cause tumors, or turn inward among the delicate circuits of the brain and set off sparks in the clinical-disorder department. One anger is not the same as another: Yelling at your husband will not make you less angry at your boss. A seriously tense person may have physical problems, such as bad digestion, but these are not necessarily helped by releasing anger. It's not necessary to express anger in order to deal with its causes. Stress-related illness appears helped most by learning how to relax.

Expressing anger has been found to lower self-esteem and can make people feel much worse about themselves. Studies on catharsis-model programs for children have shown that rather than "draining" off anger, freedom to act aggressively increases their violence. Instead of passive, happily drained children, researchers had monstrous brats on their hands.[1] People with a short fuse don't have bad tempers because they express anger too little, but because they express anger too easily. Tavris sums this up nicely when she writes that "expressing anger *while you are angry* nearly always makes you angrier."

Confronted with a squalling child or an obstinate spouse, the last thing many women need to hear is that they ought to blow off steam. We are not teakettles. Our rage can hurt. A cooling-off period or frankly squelching anger is probably a much better idea. I've found that while going into the gym hasn't helped my easily spurred anger, biting my tongue and getting out of the room has.

Once the anger is gone, talking about the problem can be a good idea. But that is a much different tactic from expressing the emotion of anger. This is one of the hardest things for me to do. As a hotheaded person, I always feel justified in wanting to tell my partner exactly what I am feeling *as* I am feeling it. The idea that I may not be justified in doing so seems like an affront to my independence.

Women frequently are told their anger is always justified—the understandable result of sexism or political injustice. In a March 1992 *Glamour* article, for example, writer Jon Tevlin asserts that women today "see many reasons to be furious," including pay inequities, rollbacks in reproductive rights, and domestic abuse. All this leads to the "basis for a cumulative anger that affects both broader social relationships and personal contacts between women and men."

While politically inspired anger can be valid, it is a stretch to portray all female anger as a reaction to oppression. As my friend dealing with her colicky infant could tell you, this is not always the case.

Of all the messages about female anger, what puzzles me the most is the one that says we should stop feeling guilty about getting mad. There are many circumstances in which guilt seems a normal response to anger—it is a mechanism that stops us from committing violence. Perhaps my perspective is faulty, but it seems to me guilt-free anger doesn't recognize our strength as much as diminish it. Why should anyone bother taking our anger seriously if it isn't important enough to be regulated by guilt?

In the cultural treatment of anger, it appears that women can't win. If we don't express anger, we are told we suffer from a syndrome and our self-esteem will suffer. But if we do express anger, it is said to be evidence of some underlying problem, such as childhood trauma or discrimination.

Labeling female anger the symptom of one sickness or another misses the point. Most people who have a problem with anger are usually perfectly normal people, and they get angry about perfectly normal things. Cooking and cleaning, sex, money, and children all come in high on surveys on marital disputes for both sexes.

As with many women, controlling my anger has been a terrible struggle at times. I feel there must be something wrong with me—to get so mad so easily. Fluttering against a wall of indifference seems worse than the firm moral lines men are given to obey or to cross. Those lines at least recognize the severity of men's anger. Denied social recognition for our ability to do harm, how many women will up the ante: yell louder, scream harder?

Feelings of powerlessness are, interestingly, some of the most powerful motivators to aggression. Wife abusers, for instance, tend to be men who feel little control in their lives. Nothing makes a person angrier than feeling incidental, and yet this is exactly what happens to women when they are mad.

In boxing, they say anger will make you lose. It's a silly saying, but it's true. Most of the time, anger does make us lose. It makes us lose when we find ourselves on the verge of striking our children, throwing things at our husbands, screaming, crying in rage, or saying things we will eternally regret.

It will continue to make us lose, especially inside the home, where the twin issues of child abuse and domestic violence—committed by women as well as men—show that women's anger is not isolated or inconsequential, but a significant social problem.

Five

THE MYTH OF THE MATERNAL INSTINCT: THE UNDEREXAMINED PROBLEM OF CHILD ABUSE COMMITTED BY WOMEN

The first time I saw children boxing, I was wrenched emotionally back to grade school, flooded with memories of being set upon by bullies.

Boys start training in amateur boxing at age eight or younger. In competition matches, these little paperweights are amazing—all fury and flailing fists. Some demonstrate surprising skill.

It took time for me to understand that for most of these boys, boxing is just another sport, the same as baseball or school wrestling. Their efforts in the ring have nothing to do with playground humiliations and childhood power struggles.

In the gym, boys and men are treated alike. Boxing reduces people to bodies and sizes. Though minors under sixteen are prohibited from competing against those seventeen and older, age is less an issue in sparring than weight and experience.

So when I was asked to spar with a child, I knew that it was simply because I was the smallest person around. Any fighter should spar with someone close to his or her own size.

The boy I was asked to spar with was about twelve. He still had the slim form of a grade schooler. He wasn't exactly a child, but he certainly wasn't an adult.

I felt torn. Like everyone else, I know that hitting children is a crime. I believe any violence against children is wrong. The idea of stepping into the ring and actually striking a child, even softly and with a padded glove, set up a visceral, gripping reaction. I looked over and saw a child on the verge of adolescence, and I remembered my youngest brother at that time, how sweet and terribly insecure he was. If there was a time to decide what I was doing was wrong, it was then. Is sparring a child abusive? Do the men have the same fear sparring me?

I should be completely honest. I was less concerned about the prospect of sparring with a child than I thought I should be. I had become so accustomed to these young boxers that I did not see them as children, but as other fighters. I knew this particular boy loves the sport and looks forward to getting into the ring. The idea of shaming him by refusing to spar seemed somehow worse than punching him.

So I did it.

He launched his blows delicately, but it was immediately clear that he was actually the better fighter. He had a clean, long jab and a graceful, popping ease of movement.

But when I smacked him with my own jab midway into the first round, a spigot opened in his nose. A nosebleed. Within moments, our gloves transferred the blood everywhere. My arms and shirt were smeared with it. A splatter flew down my legs and over my shoes. His lower face was wet with blood. It got in his eyelashes, coated my arms.

I knew intellectually that it was only a tiny blood vessel that burst, a minute and unimportant thing: the smallest wound in the head will bleed copiously, but can be staunched easily with a Q-tip. Still, I had to force myself to feel detached from the vision and sensation of blood, the knowledge that he was still only a child. I was afraid that if I felt guilty he would see it in my eyes.

When the round ended, his coach pressed a towel against the kid's nose, and everyone shrugged about his being a "bleeder," and how this was too bad for him, but maybe a doctor could fix it somehow. The kid seemed to take it in stride, annoyed his nose had a habit of springing leaks.

By the time we were into our third round, the bleeding had tapered off, and we were back to working on fundamentals. Nobody, including me, was upset that an adult had bloodied a child. The kid's coach critiqued his performance from the side of the ring. All around us the sounds of the gym were at their usual deafening roar: fighters hitting bags, doing crunches and rolls, grunting in exertion.

I've hesitated to tell this story, knowing that many people—including myself before I started boxing—would be horrified that an adult would get in the ring with someone as young as twelve, especially when the outcome is as graphic as a bloody nose.

I can't help but compare it to an incident that happened a week later. One of the fighters' wives was in the visitors' section trying to corral her two young children. Suddenly, the roar of the gym was split with an unexpected, gut-wrenching sound: the sound of a face being struck by bare hand. *I told you to shut up,* the mother yelled, as her child's face, quickly reddening, reeled backward from the slap. Into the censorious silence that gripped the gym, a full wail of pain and fear followed.

My sparring a twelve-year-old is not typical violence against children—that woman's hard slap was. For some, my act may seem worse, because it was coldly executed, where her violence was in anger and unplanned.

For women to act violently against children seems doubly wrong. We aren't just adults, we're women—and women are supposed to have "maternal instincts," programmed from the womb to protect and care for children. If children are attacked, women will supposedly risk life and limb to protect them. If children are hurt, women will do anything to see their tormentors punished. Everyone knows the image of the mama bear protecting her cubs.

Yet many women are violent against children. The unfortunate and ugly truth is child abuse is one of the most common forms of violence in our culture, and women are responsible for most of it.

According to state agency reports on child abuse, women are involved in twice as many incidents as men.[1] Altogether, in 1993 an estimated 2.3 million children were the subject of one or more reports of maltreatment in the United States.[2] Experts believe this is only a fraction of the total.

Of course, most mothers do not abuse their children— and neither do most fathers. But our notions about women's supposed pacifistic, maternal nature lead us to ignore a tremendous amount of violence perpetrated by women, against some of society's most helpless members.

No matter what their philosophical or political stance, just about everyone believes in the sanctity of motherhood. Women's responsibility in mothering is so crucial to our culture that it has taken on a romanticized life of its own, with a mythology built up around the belief that women are inherently protective and loving.

Liberals can be just as adamant as conservatives in this idealization of women's maternal side. Much liberal thought is grounded in the belief that society needs a model for a less violent future, and the ideals of motherhood fit the bill perfectly. We have yet to separate the idea of social progress from gender. Whether we dream of going forward to a nonviolent future or back to the days of "family values," beliefs in female nonaggression remain the model of our dreams of a better world. Anything that threatens this vision of motherhood can be considered sacrilegious.

The accepted wisdom is that only men beat children, while women use milder forms of violence like hand-slapping. But social scientists, law enforcement officers, and social workers will tell you that women are just as likely to engage in severe violent behavior. "[M]others are at least as likely as fathers to use even the more serious forms of violence, such as kicks, bites, punches, and beatings," write Murray Straus, Richard Gelles, and Suzanne Steinmetz in their book *Behind Closed Doors: Violence in the American Family.*

Behind Closed Doors is based on the 1975 National Family Violence survey. Conducted by the Family Research Laboratory at the University of New Hampshire, this highly regarded examination into violence within families has been conducted twice more, in 1985 and 1992. Each time the researchers have found that women are just as violent as men within the home, if not more so.

Women who beat and hurt children are not suffering from a defect in a maternal instinct gene. Many are parents without resources, and others are dealing with severe, uncompromising stress. More rarely, some may suffer from the lovely-sounding but deadly disorder "Munchausen Syndrome by Proxy," in which parents hurt their own children to gain attention.

Most abusers, however, appear to be normal women who have trouble controlling their anger.

It makes sense that those women inclined to violence—whether through design or disturbance—target children, for children are the victims they have access to.

Tilly is a woman who agreed to talk to me frankly about her violent behavior toward her child, provided I didn't use her or her daughter's actual name. She is a smart, successful woman with a career, nice home and marriage, and a beautiful little girl I'll call Patricia—everything that defines a well-adjusted woman in our society.

Tilly has a hard time managing her temper with her child. So far, her violence has been confined to slapping and spanking, as well as a few occasions when she brutally pushed the girl aside or bodily picked her up and moved her into her room. "Those little arms," she says, "like sticks. You could just snap them, like *that*."

Tilly's violence toward her child is not severe enough to qualify as criminal abuse. For many people, slapping and spanking are perfectly acceptable forms of discipline.

But Tilly doesn't believe children should be hit, and so when she acts violently, it is not because of a calm wish to discipline but because of savage anger. It is the emotion that drives her aggression that troubles her: the knowledge that she tries to use physical or emotional pain to control a child she loves.

When we talked, I mentioned a recent case in which a parent was shaking his child and accidentally killed him (that quick snap of the neck—it is remarkably easy to kill a young child this way). Tilly visibly paled. Accidental harm resulting from her violence is a possibility that appears to worry her deeply.

Tilly comes from a violent family. Her mother would slap her in the face when angry. The children learned violence from their mother, and so sibling battles took murderous routes. Now an adult, Tilly finds herself kicking the cat when angry or easily resorting to striking out. "For me, the problem is when I am so enraged, I don't know how to step back," she says. "I don't have tools to deal with anger."

An effort at counseling didn't work. "The counselor said I was overstressed." Tilly gives a dry laugh. "Any mom, even a stay-at-home-all-the-time mom, is going to get overstressed sometimes." The therapist didn't give her any helpful suggestions, Tilly says, only the kind of stress-reduction tips a fourth grader would know.

Stress is bound to build sooner or later. What to do when the tips don't work and anger rises? The ideal of the maternal instinct can act as a barrier to acquiring tools women need to cope with children. If you really love your kids, the text of public conversation to mothers reads, you won't hit them. End of discussion. Who needs tools when instincts are supposedly doing your job for you?

Tilly believes that sports and other approved forms of male aggression allow men to learn that fighting is sometimes acceptable, even necessary, but that it has to stay within bounds. Women, she says, miss out on learning "that it's okay to be frustrated." In her mind, this leaves women without any boundaries at all, and in particular leaves women such as herself feeling as if their anger exists in a vacuum, unnoticed unless they really go over the edge. Then society will step in and, in horror, condemn them as unnatural mothers, unworthy of raising children.

Tilly is still, I think, a good mother. She loves her daughter, and even as she wrestles with anger, she is a caring parent. Her moral sense is well developed enough that she knows when she is doing wrong.

"I feel like a monster," Tilly says. "There have been times I have walked behind Patricia and thought, I would like to kick you to the moon. Now, you tell me, what kind of mom wants their child to live in fear?"

There are many moms whose children live in fear of them—honest, ripe, constant fear. There are thousands of mothers who make Tilly's slaps and pushing look positively benign.

State child-protection agencies work firsthand with the results of women's violence against children. The cases are depressing: children with burn marks on their hands from cigarettes, bald spots where hair was torn out, bruises on their bodies from beatings with sticks or whatever weapon was close at hand; toddlers who are the size of starved monkeys, diagnosed with "failure to thrive" because of chronic neglect; children who look fine but whose deadened expressions hide a history of sexual abuse, committed by women as well as by men.

More than any other evidence, violence against children turns biological theories of aggression on their head. If men had more of a genetic predisposition to violence, or women had special instincts against harming others, these traits would be reflected in the statistics. But similar stresses and the ability to hide violence within the family elicits similar responses. Women, in the midst of anger, find themselves hitting, shaking, and beating.

Women's physical violence against children is often overlooked. Many articles have been written about the lack of attention paid to abuse; it seems that police and neighbors are more willing to report cases of neglect than of physical violence. Of reported maltreatment, one-fourth of the cases are for physical abuse, about a half are for neglect, and the rest are for sexual abuse, prenatal drug use, and abandonment.[3]

Neglect can be a form of violence in and of itself. Many neglect cases are marked by starvation, malnutrition, and disease, as in one case in my area where a drug-addicted mother left her infant in a cardboard box on the floor for days, unfed and unwashed. When authorities found the infant, it was little more than skin and bones, barely alive.

The ambiguous line between corporal punishment and abuse helps explain why so many mothers act violently. To be blunt, they can get away with it. Most Americans still believe spanking is acceptable, and quite a few still use switches, paddles, and belts.

With aggression against children condoned under some circumstances, it's easier to use violence in times of frustration. A 1994 Gallup poll found that nearly one in eight respondents had been "punched or kicked or choked" by a parent during childhood.[4]

People sometimes say, "My parents spanked me, and I turned out fine," or something similar. This may be true. But the fact is, corporal punishment is intended to hurt, and such a deliberate action designed to inflict pain can't be anything but aggression. The same assault on an adult is considered criminal.

How often is aggression toward children really based in calm reason? Or how often do we let ourselves go ahead and hurt a child because, like Tilly, we get mad, upset, in a rage? Because we can? The women we see dragging their children behind them in public, slapping a reddened face, threatening and bullying are aggressive, violent women. So are the thousands of women who do such things in private. When you consider how many women struggle with the propensity for acting violently against their children, female aggression no longer seems unusual. It is revealed as remarkably common.

Nothing represents an unnatural woman more than the sexual abuser, in whom violence intersects with predatory sexuality, and nothing challenges our ideal of the maternal instinct more. Just to mention women's behavior in this realm is controversial, far more so than with physical abuse.

It does appear that women commit less sexual abuse than men. Depending on the study, the numbers fluctuate. Estimates of sexual abuse committed by women range from five percent of all cases to one-third or more.[5]

According to one child-welfare worker I spoke with, approximately one in five sexually abused children is victimized by a woman. This 20 percent figure strikes me as plausible. Even if the rate is much lower, sex abuse by women still deserves to be taken seriously if we hope to help both victims and offenders.

There has been little research on female sex offenders. In studies on sex abusers, women are frequently excluded, and in surveys of the general population, questions are often designed to elicit information on abuse by men, not women.

Many people picture a female sex offender as the proverbial older woman—an attractive divorcée initiating a willing adolescent boy into the pleasures of sex, a widow looking for solace, a sexy neighbor out for a good time. Fantasy movies—such as *Summer of '42* or *Risky Business*, with the gawky teenage boy meeting the sexually active older woman and pleasurably discovering the ways of love— demonstrate how we like to wink at sexual abuse by women. The scenario does not seem half as reprehensible as Humbert Humbert molesting Lolita and leaving her to cry herself to sleep night after night. The male sex offender is thought of as a dirty lech, a child molester, a man who will rape his own daughter or fondle frightened little boys behind the bushes. The female sex offender is seen as a movie star past the age of thirty.

But the reality of sexual abuse by women is just as sordid as abuse by men. Sometimes it involves penetration with objects, mutual masturbation, oral sex, and sex acts with infants.

One study of sixteen female sex offenders in a Minnesota program gives a detailed clinical portrait of such women.[6] Only one of the women in the Minnesota study came close to fitting the classic "teacher/student" profile. This story of a woman having sex with twelve-year-old boys, however, sounds anything but romantic in its sad details of an emotionally stunted, overweight woman who played spin the bottle with neighborhood children.

Most of the other female offenders in this treatment program committed severe, intrusive sexual abuse, often to their own young children over long periods of time. One mother began "rubbing and inserting her finger into their [her daughters'] vaginas and having oral sex with them," beginning in infancy and continuing until they were three years old.

Another mother made her daughters masturbate her, using a vibrator, while she fantasized about "the perfect man." Some had sex with children in conjunction with men. Others acted alone.

What is striking about the women sexual abusers in this study is how easily they used their position as caretakers to abuse children. The abuse sometimes stayed hidden for years, and it was often extremely manipulative, such as mothers using threats of abandonment to keep their children from telling.

The women in this study either came to the attention of the law or turned themselves in. They were probably engaged in more long-term abuse than most offenders.

Some researchers have suggested that less obvious kinds of sexual abuse committed by women, such as giving frequent enemas, playing pretend breast-feeding, taking showers together and sleeping with older children, may be more common than we think. Such acts usually don't result in reported offenses and prosecution. While the same could easily be true for fathers, it's possible that women's role as primary caregivers allows them greater latitude to aggress this way.

In examining sexual abuse committed by women, it becomes painfully clear that the denial of its occurrence is exceedingly hard on the victims. Those searching for help tell of authorities who refuse to believe them, thus robbing them of the assistance they need—assistance that may, in some cases, prevent victims from becoming future offenders.

One such story is told by an Australian female sex offender in a book entitled *From Victim to Offender*. This woman grew up in an abusive household herself, with a mother who was clearly disturbed. The mother tortured her two daughters with sadistic sexual practices, such as forcing objects up their vaginas. When the two sisters tried to report the abuse to the police, they weren't believed. The abuse continued for years.

After finally leaving home, this woman tried to create a normal life. She married and had twin sons. But her husband left her, and soon she fell into a state of depression. Within a short period, she found herself repeating the sexual abuse of her childhood. Only now *she* was the perpetrator, with her two young sons as her victims. She writes that she never expected to become a sex abuser herself.

Sickened by her own actions, she went to the local police station. There she announced she was molesting her own children, and she asked to be arrested. The response was disbelief. "When the youthful constable stopped laughing and realised I was both sober and serious, he sent for the duty sergeant who declared he had 'never heard of anything quite like it. . . .' " After chewing on the end of his pencil for a moment, the sergeant actually told her to go home, and he advised her to "talk it over with your family doctor."

No one interviewed her children or followed up on her confession. It was only after she pursued the matter, demanding arrest and treatment, that a counselor took her seriously and that her sons were finally removed from her home. The two boys were placed in foster care, and at the time of her writing, she was undergoing treatment, in the hope they would be returned to her.

While this woman's story may be unusual in its depiction of police ineptitude, the denial of both her victimization and her abuse is not.

The most well-intentioned scientists can allow political perspectives to override actual findings. According to *From Victim to Offender*, when an Australian phone-in survey showed that over one-third of the cases of sexual abuse involved female offenders, "some of the female organizers rejected the information and sought alternative explanations to account for the results. The explanation which best fitted their own ideology was that the calls were a 'hoax' perpetrated by paedophiles to implicate women. . . ."

It seems to me that addressing sexual abuse by women is hampered by the popular view that molestation is a reflection of masculine misuse of power. Offenders are referred to as "he" and victims as "she" (though male victims are getting greater recognition).

Female perpetrators are frequently said to sexually abuse only when forced to by men, or when acting out victimization of their own. The possibility that women sex offenders may use sexuality in as predatory a manner as men is given scant attention.

I think it demands more. Several of the women in the Minnesota study spoke of feeling aroused by the sexual abuse they perpetrated. Like male offenders, their words hint at feelings of power, domination, and control. One woman who had sexually abused her four daughters by inserting her fingers into their vaginas and having oral sex with them said the abuse made her feel "sexually aroused" and "very powerful."

Another woman, given the name Grace for the study, was eighteen when she began sexually abusing. Her victim was her nine-year-old nephew. "He would be playing with cards, Legos or listening to music. . . . I would then reach over [and] . . . put my hands inside his pants, then I'd ask him to take his pants off," she said. "I would ask him to lay down. He would. I would then suck on his penis. He would get scared and tense. . . ." Grace said she felt aroused by this abuse. Her arousal seemed heightened by the little boy's fear.

Ignoring women sex offenders because they are a minority of the total number or simply because they are women makes little sense to me. "Why is it so difficult to understand female-initiated child sexual abuse?" the woman sex offender in *From Victim to Offender* writes. "Is the problem ignored because people think that abuse by women is less damaging (and therefore less important) than abuse by men? Is it because we perceive the penis as *the* dangerous weapon and, without one, the female offender must, of necessity, be less harmful?" Or is it because, as English writer Alix Kirsta asks in her book *Deadlier Than the Male: Violence and Aggression in Women:* "In taking female sexual abuse seriously, are we guilty of the ultimate and final heresy, the destruction of the myth of motherhood?"

It doesn't make mothering a less reliable, ingrained, honest, and trustworthy human trait to understand it requires effort. Just as an adoptive parent can form a bond as deep as any birth parent, whether we care—or commit harm—is not biologically determined; it is a matter of choice. And sometimes it can be a difficult daily challenge.

The days when women stayed home with their children—and were expected to be teacher, baby-sitter, nurse, and guidance counselor rolled into one—are gone. Women today work, and so we find ourselves shifting some parenting over to schools, child-care workers, fathers, and others in the community. I personally consider this progress, and better for families, who are given a broader base of support and services.

But at the same time we need to make parenting more of a community effort (which requires open discussion of just what parenting is), we want to retain the idea of the family as sacred, above social and governmental intervention. We especially want to retain our rosy picture of motherhood, even as the doors are being opened and once-hidden abuse is made more obvious. In recent years, a glut of memoirs and confessionals detailing abuse by mothers may be evidence that social changes are making women's violence in the home far more visible.

In the realm of child abuse, assumptions that women are nonaggressive are transparently false and sadly destructive. They push abuse into the private realm, leaving it shrouded in mystery and the abusers removed from the help they need.

This denial is even more pronounced in perceptions of domestic violence. In all our very public talk about battery and abuse, women's actions against husbands and lesbian partners remain ridiculed, silenced, and misunderstood.

Six

VIOLENCE IN RELATIONSHIPS: IT'S NOT ALWAYS A ONE-WAY STREET

Making small talk one day while getting ready to spar, I asked a fighter about the small mouse under his eye. I assumed he'd say he'd gotten the raised black bruise in the ring. Instead, he laughed, somewhat embarrassed and oddly proud, and said he'd gotten it from his wife. "She's got a temper," he admitted, and rolled his eyes, laughing. "That's why I don't have a problem with you girls in the ring," he said, and cuffed the side of my headgear with an open hand before striding away, leaving me to stand there confused.

Is domestic violence against men different from domestic violence against women? Even in cases where men suffer injury and degradation, many would say yes. The boxer treated his black eye with humor, but I don't know how deeply his feelings of nonchalance ran. I've heard women hit by their husbands talk in similar mixed tones of pride and shame, wanting to believe that an act of disrespect was a sign of caring.

It's hard to picture a boxer being victimized by a woman. For that matter, it's hard to think of most men being victimized by women. This is not a culture that takes violence committed by women against men seriously. We laugh at the thought, picturing a woman pummeling a man with ineffectual fists.

Yet women do act violently toward their mates. "I come from a family in which my old man used to beat us," a man who had left an abusive relationship wrote me about his marriage. "Things were fine for a year or so, but then violence began creeping into the relationship, and I internalized it, thinking I deserve to be hit. . . . Anyway, I'm glad to feel the security of not being beaten every time I mess up, and I hope my ex-wife is battling her demons. . . ."

I believe part of the reason this scenario is so difficult to accept is because our understanding of domestic violence itself tends to be inaccurate. We equate *domestic violence* with *battery*.

There are public message billboards near my home that feature a graphic photo of a model-beautiful woman with a bruised and battered face, a half-closed black eye (IT IS YOUR BUSINESS the billboard insists). This is the face of domestic violence we are accustomed to: women who are battered to the point of hospitalization; women who live in fear of extremely violent husbands. The opening salvo of a July 4, 1994, *Time* article relates the story of a woman whose husband beat her so viciously, she lost most of her hearing. Violence in relationships, to read this article, happens only to women, and it happens to millions of us, a life-threatening epidemic of violence that "often involves severe physical or psychological damage." The article closes with a description of the same battered woman, cowering in a shelter as her psychotic husband stalks her.

Such pathological attacks certainly do occur. But they represent only a tiny fraction of domestic violence.

The bulk of the numbers so frequently cited for domestic violence—the estimates of millions—are for what researchers call "minor violence," such as couples who get in pushing matches, grab each other, or slap on rare occasions. Such acts are not frequent or severe enough to be called battery.

When both sexes engage in such fighting, experts call it "mutual violence."

A woman I'll call Laura told me of a fight she and her husband got into. She couldn't even remember what had started it—it might have been chores, or just stress from work spilling over. Soon both were hashing over old grievances, insulting each other, and yelling. The yelling escalated until, more angry than she could bear, she began throwing things at him. Plates and other dishes shattered against the walls and floors. At first too shocked to move, her husband ducked out of the way of a flying plate and marched up to her, twisted her wrist, and forced her to drop the dish she was holding.

Later, both were distressed at their behavior. Neither of them, she said, wanted anything similar to happen ever again.

Laura's story is not going to make it onto a billboard. It doesn't raise much concern because it doesn't fall into a neat pattern of violence, a clear gender line between abuser and victim. It doesn't represent the gratuitous and meaningless violence of a wife beater; instead, it shows the kind of embarrassing aggression many of us can envision ourselves taking part in. And because we can imagine ourselves throwing a plate in anger, like Laura, or twisting someone's wrist in response, like her husband, we tend to want to pull the covers up over such incidents, declaring them private altercations or personal idiosyncrasies, best left to the secret life of marriage.

I think minor domestic violence like this is still important. Laura pointed out that one of them could easily have gotten hurt. What if one of her plates had met its mark and opened a gash on his head? What if he had accidentally broken her wrist? What was a noninjurious fight could easily have put someone into the hospital.

Besides, the sense of violation and mistrust following such an emotional explosion was not healthy for either of them. Laura says they weren't sure what to make of the incident. What did it mean? Were they exaggerating the importance of their actions? Or were they doomed to an escalating future of abuse?

With our only model of domestic violence that of male battery, the answer given to women is usually the same: Leave. We aren't quite sure what to do about incidents in which aggression is mild or the blame is shared. The easy declarations don't work. There isn't an agreed-upon way of dealing with such altercations.

That women as well as men push, shove, slap, and, in rarer instances, beat with fists or use weapons does not make for an epidemic of battered husbands, as some commentators have suggested. What it does mean is that women are not always the nonaggressive partners in relationships, as we have assumed in the past.

Like others who have addressed women's aggression in relationships, I worry that I will be accused of downplaying wife battery or endorsing domestic violence. I am not doing either. This is a highly emotional topic, one driven more by heartfelt convictions than cold science, and my examination of the research is not meant to demean the raw trauma of abuse.

I do believe we need to get past a simplistic view of domestic violence as male-on-female, a one-way street ending at the morgue. It denies help to women like Laura, whose story doesn't conform to the accepted view, and it gives a false understanding of human aggression, especially in our private lives. The reality of domestic violence is that it seems more likely to cross a spectrum—with each case different—than to fall into such tidy patterns, such a dichotomy of emotion, dividing cleanly along lines of gender.

Any of us can find violence creeping into our relationships, and in the midst of an argument we may suddenly discover that abusiveness is not the provenance of the wife batterer or as foreign as what is depicted on those graphic billboards, but that it is a great deal closer to home.

First, the statistics. The National Family Violence surveys—the same studies that uncovered high rates of child abuse by women—also found startling rates of female domestic violence.[1]

The respondents in this survey were asked specifically about what kinds of violent behavior they displayed in fights with their spouses. Did they push, shove, or grab? Did they slap? Choke or use a weapon? What about biting and kicking?

Women admitted to doing all the above.

In the 1985 survey, for instance, roughly one in eight men and women admitted using some form of aggression against a partner. Women were actually slightly more likely than men to engage in severely violent behavior like biting, kicking, hitting with an object, and threatening with guns or knives.

The study's researchers go to pains to point out that men are more likely to inflict injury, probably due to their greater size. Three percent of the assaults by husbands caused injury, while less than 1 percent of the assaults by wives did.

That 97 percent of assaults by men—and 99 percent of assaults by women—don't cause injury shouldn't lead us to shrug them off. Advocates for abused women have long pointed out that making injury the prerequisite for intervention can lead to situations in which police don't respond, violence spirals out of control, and a victim has to be dead before she (or he) sees justice.

One common criticism of these particular surveys is that they didn't capture the context and meaning of violence. A push by a woman, critics reason, is bound to be much different from a push by a man. In her book *Woman-Battering*, Mildred Daley Pagelow scoffs that "a kick with an open-toed sandal administered under a bridge table and an angry kick from a pointed western boot are vastly different. . . ."

This perspective, with delicately attired bridge players juxtaposed against violent cowboys, doesn't gel with the answers from women themselves. It seems unlikely to me that women misinterpreted the questions to be inquiring about shushing kicks during card games, love slaps, or other forms of playful aggression.

In addition, in an interview, Murray Straus, coauthor of the surveys, professor, and codirector of the Family Research Laboratory at the University of New Hampshire, confirmed that over half (53 percent) of the women said they struck the first blow during fights. This finding also helps answer the second common criticism leveled at the surveys, which is that women must be acting out of self-defense. If that was the case, not so many would be the first to hit.

If it isn't self-defense or playful aggression, then what is it? There are dozens of other studies that also show women can be aggressive in relationships.[2] All hint at the same reason: Women can be just as violent as men, period.

No place is this better illustrated than among lesbian couples. Studies strongly suggest that there is just as much violence among lesbian couples as among heterosexual ones.[3]

Lesbian domestic violence challenges the stereotype that women cannot or will not strike another person, or that when they do, their violence is ineffective. "The hospital repaired two broken wrists, two broken thumbs, a broken ankle, bruised ribs, black eyes and various cuts and bruises, but they never asked how I came to receive these regular injuries," one lesbian woman battered by her partner asserted.[4]

While studies show that women are just as aggressive within relationships, domestic violence crime reports are still overwhelmingly made up of female victims. Researcher Murray Straus observes that police reports may not capture the majority of domestic violence, since while many people think it is wrong for their husband or wife to throw a lamp at them, few think it is a crime per se. What violence does make its way into police reports is more likely to be battery, and here again women are more likely to be injured.

There is also the stigma attached to being beaten by a woman. Not many men are willing to identify themselves as victims of female violence.

A selective culling of facts occurs in the press with regard to domestic violence. A January 15, 1995, *New York Times* article, based on statistics from the 1985 National Family Violence survey, stated that "wife battery" is underestimated. No mention was made that half the perpetrators of domestic violence uncovered in the study were women. A reader was likely to mistakenly conclude the study found no evidence of female violence in the home.

This misrepresentation happens constantly. Murray Straus tells of some instances where scientists have suppressed their own findings.[5]

Even some of the well-accepted statistics we are assailed with are misrepresentations of domestic violence also involving women perpetrators.

We have all heard the claim that a woman is "battered by her husband every eighteen seconds." The Federal Bureau of Investigation arrived at this number by extrapolating from a 1975 National Family Violence survey estimate that 2 million people had been "beaten up by his or her spouse" that year. After dividing the figure by the number of seconds in the year, the FBI dropped the "his or her," and the victims were presented as exclusively women.[6]

Of course, a good portion of the victims were men. A more accurate claim would be that every eighteen seconds in 1975, a man or woman was beaten up by his or her spouse.

But that doesn't have quite the same ring to it.

What does women's domestic violence look like?

There is a condom ad designed to appeal to teenagers. Every day, a pretty girl encounters a boy on the street. He tries to make clumsy moves on her, calling her "baby." She hauls off and punches him—*whap*—right in the kisser. Then she blows off the finger dust with sexy lips. Finally, he goes out and buys a condom and waves the magical receptacle. "You're learning," she coos, and then hauls off and throws a tremendous right hand, knocking him once more to the ground. From the ground, he mutters, "I think she likes me."

I don't want to be the kind of dour person who takes umbrage at every commercial. Slapstick violence *can* be funny, and I think many depictions of female aggression, like that particular commercial, are. But they shouldn't eclipse information of a more concrete nature.

Like women's abuse of children, the real face of female domestic violence is not so charming. I used to live near a couple who fit the profile of mutual violence. They acted like speed addicts, out working on their project cars at three in the morning, drinking beer at noon in a desperate attempt to come down, then erupting into abuse against each other as their tempers flared—throwing things, slamming doors, screaming threats. The neighbors would call the police, but neither partner was interested in pressing charges. That woman gave as good as she got.

I don't think this couple's pattern of violence is unusual in domestic violence. A friend who works in a shelter for abused women says she believes most of her clients are caught up in mutually destructive relationships, where both partners are enmeshed in negative behaviors. Many of us can think of couples who fight on equal terms, and women who are fearless when enraged. Sometimes violent couples follow unspoken rules of fighting. Fighting may mean either spouse can slap or push but not use a closed fist. This is not to say these relationships are healthy, only that their violence is mutual.

There is little sympathy for a man who is attacked by his wife. On the Oregon coast, a woman was accused of sneaking up on her newlywed husband and bludgeoning him with a tire iron. The state's largest newspaper treated the incident as high entertainment, with the headline HUSBAND SURVIVES THE LUMPS AND BUMPS OF A NEW MARRIAGE, but readers found a decidedly unfunny story of a man with broken fingers from trying to ward off the blows of a brutal attack.[7] The wife was later convicted of attempted murder and sentenced to several years in prison. It was alleged she had tried to murder him for his money.

Men assaulted by their wives may find a complete lack of services. In a study on domestic police calls in Detroit, one man was hospitalized after his wife stabbed him in the chest, barely missing his lungs. Not only did the police refuse to arrest her; they wouldn't even remove her from the home.[8]

I do believe that women are more likely than men to be subjected to the ongoing severe violence that characterizes battery. Being trapped changes the tone and meaning of violence, and women do get trapped in relationships more often, economically and socially. Children make it especially difficult for many women to leave battering husbands.

In my eyes, women are also pressured more to "stick it out" when things get bad, even at the cost of accepting victimization. In addition, there is the crucial issue of strength. While some women are just as large and strong as their partners, most are at a physical disadvantage.

But men can feel trapped, too. Many men would never strike their wives, even in response to being attacked. Some men who have been in relationships with violent women tell how they were afraid to leave, lest they lose beloved children, social status, parental approval, or standing in their religious community. Just like abused women, they will say they loved their wives, even as they feared their anger, and describe the "honeymoon" following violent episodes, where all is forgiven.

Many people, however, believe that battered women are completely different from abused men—psychologically, culturally, and socially.

An arena of law and social services has been carved out for abused women, unlike abused men. Even the courts treat the two much differently, such as with the battered woman's syndrome. According to proponents of this legal defense, women who kill their abusive mates are driven by fear and a sort of broken paralysis—what Lenore Walker, an activist who pioneered the use of the term *battered woman's syndrome*, calls "learned helplessness."

In some cases, the defense seems reasonable. A woman is terrified for years by a battering husband, until finally, convinced she will die at his hands, she kills him as he sleeps. But in other cases, the argument is stretched to implausible lengths. Walker has testified in cases in which women hired hit men to kill their husbands.

Before Cynthia Lynn Coffman met up with the battered woman's syndrome defense, she went on a killing spree with her boyfriend. The child of middle-class Catholics, Coffman was an attractive woman who left home at age seventeen, pregnant. Eventually, she hooked up with a career criminal named James Gregory Marlow. Marlow called himself "the Folsom Wolf." Some of the tattoos adorning his frame were insignia of the white supremacist prison gang Aryan Brotherhood.

Apparently, Coffman fell madly in love with Marlow. The two were unofficially married in a biker ceremony while sitting atop a Harley-Davidson motorcycle. Coffman had "Property of Folsom Wolf" tattooed on her buttocks, and in 1986, a cross-country killing spree, fueled by injections of crystal methamphetamine, began. Exactly how many the two murdered is open to debate. There were at least two victims.

The couple started in California, where they kidnapped a young woman. Coffman watched while Marlow raped and sodomized the woman, and then she helped him strangle her. The next victim was found facedown in a motel bathtub, raped, beaten, and strangled with a towel.

After their arrest—which included a dramatic police sweep through a mountain range—Coffman continued to express her undying love for Marlow. She wrote him prison letters with swastikas dotting her *i*'s.

Lenore Walker testified that Coffman suffered from battered woman's syndrome. "I testified that Sarah [Walker does not use Coffman's or Marlow's real name, but the case is clear from details] had been George's victim, too, even though she had been unaware of his psychological hold over her," Walker writes in her book *Terrifying Love*. She portrays Coffman as a severely battered, frightened woman who had been under a "brainwashing" spell by her psychopathic partner and was "forced" into participation in kidnapping, sexual assault, and murder.

To me, this case highlights the dangers—and appeal—of popular views on domestic violence. Cynthia Coffman was a woman who went on a rampage of sex murders with a man. She partook in the crimes and showed little remorse afterward. The April 26, 1992, issue of the *Los Angeles Times* said she appeared in good spirits in prison, "smiling and laughing with ease during a two-hour interview." A district attorney described her as a smart, manipulative person, adding that the jury thought she was the cleverer of the two. Depicting her as having acted in some twisted form of self-defense is forcing the proverbial square peg in a round hole. Yet that is precisely what happens in cases where women's aggression flies in the face of conventional views of female passivity.

In her book *It's All the Rage: Crime and Culture*, social critic Wendy Kaminer makes a strong point. A "claim of victimization is not a claim of innocence," she writes.

I think Kaminer captures a fundamental problem with our views on female aggression: a lack of recognition that one can be both victim *and* aggressor. Maybe Marlow did batter Coffman. Yet that doesn't mean that Coffman was an unwilling participant in their crimes. Maybe she even took great pleasure in her violence. The most hideous victimization doesn't erase human failings or corrupt desires; a person victimized may actually be more prone to strike out, more likely to suffer a lack of empathy, more likely to be emotionally stunted. I believe we can find a way to balance an understanding of the difficulties in women's—and men's—lives without denying their accountability, or denying our compassion.

Coffman was convicted. She is currently on California's death row.

There is the old saw that violence begets violence. Couples who are abusive are more likely to strike their children. Women who are beaten by their husbands may turn around and batter their kids. Of the battered women studied by Walker, discussed in her book *The Battered Woman Syndrome*, over one-fourth abused their children.

Violence within families spreads to siblings and elderly dependents, then is passed generation to generation.

A December 12, 1994, *New York Times* article tells of the "heirloom" of violence passed along the female side of one family, culminating in a fifteen-year-old boy accused of murder. As a child, the boy watched his mother kill a boyfriend in a violent quarrel. Later accused of armed robbery, she was neglectful and abusive. He was sent to live with his grandmother, who wasn't much of an improvement. Grandma boasted of having killed several people, including the father of two of her seventeen children. When the boy was the tender age of eleven, she gave him his own pistol to carry on the streets.

At age fifteen, the legacy of family violence, learned firsthand from the women of the family, paid off. The boy shot and killed a friend during an argument.

There are many influences to family violence: unemployment, alcoholism and drug abuse, lack of basic education and impulse control.

Addressing family violence requires admitting that women, too, might have a problem—an heirloom of violence.

The same is true for the intensely complicated, hot-button issue of crime.

Seven ~

CRIMINAL WOMEN

Y ou're getting in shape," Jess told me one day as he watched with a calculating eye as I did push-ups. His words were not offered as praise, but as simple observation. I finished the set and got up, dusting the gym grime off my bare knees. I thanked Jess for the compliment, but he only grunted in acknowledgment.

Around me, men worked in studious concentration. Ernesto, a young man of Mexican descent, was shadow-boxing in front of the mirrors. His naked torso, wet with sweat, was a clean expanse of flesh tapering to a narrow waist. I watched him for a moment, noticing for the first time what he had turned his body into. He looked like the muscle man demonstrating the virtues of the Charles Atlas program. Yet he was not bulky with useless muscle, but honed—128 pounds on a short frame—with each muscle trained to serve a purpose. Like most fighters, his muscles were loose and relaxed, almost baggy on his frame. Nothing constricted; nothing bound. The reality of boxing is not power, but this relaxation: the ability to let a punch go.

Muhammad Ali used to yell "I'm so pretty. I'm so pretty." And he was. George Foreman says Ali was the only pretty fighter, but I think that sluggers with mashed faces and scarred eyebrows can be pretty in their own right. Perhaps more than swimmers with their fine flesh, the fighter's body is a work animal: a horse. Even the heavyweights, with solid slabs of fat around the middle and beefy arms, give a sense of a body simultaneously suspended in action and rooted to the canvas, working, always working.

Observing Ernesto's body, I noticed the tattoo across his back shoulder. I'd seen his tattoos before but hadn't registered them until now. Taking my jump rope back to my gym bag—which I store under the ring because there isn't a women's dressing room—I surreptitiously looked more closely at Ernesto's tattoo. I thought it said *Burnsides*, in an arching range across the skin of his back, right across the left shoulder blade.

The Mexican men of the Sandoval team, which I, too, am a member of, often sport tattoos across their backs. These are gang insignia, I think. In all likelihood, Ernesto didn't tattoo the name of his bowling team on his shoulder. He comes from Los Angeles, along with his brother Anthony, and he dresses in a current fashion among young Hispanic men: oversized, low-slung jeans and massive shirts. Everything is always immaculate, starched, including the clean line of cuff a neat inch above the ankle.

A few of the men wear hair nets, and others have carefully glossy pompadours, but Ernesto has his black hair shorn close, except for a small braided tail along the tendoned line of his neck. When we spar, he gives me a wise, knowing look. He has a square, tidy face with a long, hooking nose and caramel-colored eyes.

I get the sense that Ernesto and his brother Anthony, unlike most of the men, aren't bothered by my presence. Anthony is a rangier fellow. He looks at me straight in the face when he comes into the gym, asks how I am doing. Anthony talks to me when we spar, conversationally. He tells me when I need to try something, encourages me under his breath—"Work the body," he whispers. "Work the body."

Ernesto is silent when we spar, but he comes on like a train. Jess likes to point proudly at him and say, "He's a little bulldog." He is. He grabs ahold of your neck and doesn't let go. After one session, when Ernesto really started to come on, he asked Jess if he had been hitting me too hard. I couldn't hear Jess's reply, but it seemed to be dismissive, another grunt.

Here at Grand Avenue, Jess draws in Hispanic men. They come, having heard of him, to be under his wing for training.

Several of the men at the gym spend hours busing and driving in from Hillsboro, an outlying rural suburb where many Hispanics live. The younger boys show up fresh from school, while the older men sometimes bring their wives and children. Jess finds reason to mention when they attend community college to learn English. He speaks English to those trying to learn, in order to help them. He mentions when they are in the country alone, and how he feels sorry for them because they are alone and so poor.

The male Hispanic culture is supposed to be macho, but I have yet to find it in this vulnerable, striving group, where the men give me wide, uneasy grins when I ask for a turn at the speed bag. I feel clumsy, aware of my deficiencies: In all these months, I have never learned much Spanish, besides the question "Totally finished?" in reference to that speed bag.

I sense that, underneath his tough veneer, Ernesto is as fragile and aware as a newly hatched bird.

I say nothing about the tattoo Ernesto has across his shoulder, because there is nothing worth saying. Other fighters have tattooed lists of names—possibly of friends killed—on their arms. The names scroll in long faded charcoal lists. Some have tiny teardrops, dotted knuckles: prison tattoos.

One night, I stopped in at the neighborhood hardware store for some potting soil. I noticed that the kid behind me in line—it wasn't Ernesto, but someone else—was buying bullets. The sight of those bullets ("Full Metal Jacket" was printed on the box) made me instinctively look away.

But as I was going to my car, the young man caught up with me. "I thought I knew you—you're from the gym," he exclaimed. Another fighter from the gym waited for him in a buttercup yellow Cadillac. The two greeted me profusely.

I didn't think the bullets were for target practice—not at ten o'clock on a Saturday night. It felt strange, as if someone had lifted off the sky, to stand around in a parking lot talking to two young men I know and like and to be confronted visibly with evidence of the chasm between us. I thought about saying something about the bullets, but I would have felt condescending lecturing them.

The next time we sparred, I found myself leaning over Ernesto's shoulder as I tried desperately to punch him in the belly. He was naked above the waist again, clad only in a protective belt over blue terry-cloth trunks. His shoulders were sweaty where we made contact. Ernesto's tattoos are only part of that flesh, limited, and—in the end—only a tiny part of his story. Who can say if they have meaning? Where I thudded him on his rib, there was only iridescent skin, shiny and fragile, as soft as the underside of my arm.

Crime and men: The two fit. It makes sense that the men of the Grand Avenue boxing gym would hint of shady connections to gangs and crime. Boxing gyms are supposed to be places to keep young "at risk" men out of trouble. There isn't an equivalent for women.

We assume it is men who get into trouble, and women who suffer for it.

Male crime gets the attention, the new laws, the research funding, and the nightly news spot. Women's crime, except for the occasional story, is given short shrift, leading people to think it just doesn't happen.

Nothing could be further from the truth. Women commit crime. We commit violent crimes, petty crimes, property crimes, and workplace crimes. We rob, steal, cheat, and deal drugs. We kill our family members and, although more rarely than men, strangers. We are even serial murderers. Women commit their share of certain crimes, and a substantial portion of others.

The question of why women have historically committed fewer crimes than men has led to a hundred theories, from the sound to the silly. Central to most approaches is an unwillingness to engage with women's aggressive autonomy.

What causes some women to steal, hurt, and kill others? Are women criminals different from male criminals? How has feminism affected crime?

I once knew a woman with the nickname of Cookie. She had served time for armed robbery. I met her when I was working in a city detox facility, serving a population that was mostly homeless and sometimes criminal. She was a thin, wiry woman with unnerving pale eyes. In his novel *The Pope of Greenwich Village*, writer Vincent Patrick notes that women nicknamed Cookie are not women you would want to mess with; in this case at least, he was right. When she told me she had robbed at gunpoint, I believed her.

One night months after meeting her, I ran into Cookie in a nightclub. For some dumb reason, I made the mistake of giving her my phone number. After that, the phone would periodically ring with pleas for help making bail. I never did.

One woman named Cookie, of course, does not make for a female crime wave. As far as armed robbers go, she was unusual. About one in twelve robbery arrests is of a woman.[1] On the other hand, one in twelve is not exactly a rarity, either. While women represent a minority of most arrests, their numbers are far from inconsequential. In 1992, for instance, over 64,000 women were arrested for aggravated assault (assault involving a weapon or with intent to commit serious bodily harm or death).

With prose verging on the purple, commentators call the networks and subcultures in which much crime occurs "the criminal underbelly"—cultures that women like Cookie hail from. Bookies, gamblers, organized crime outfits, fencing operations, prostitution rings, scam artists, and drug dealers—these often occur in overlapping circles, a series of subcultures in which people move easily from one crime to another.

Such subcultures have always been thought of as male-dominated. Certainly most Mafia movies and cinematic depictions of crime, from spaghetti Westerns to modern thrillers, make women out to be window dressing for male criminals. If acknowledged, the women in such worlds are usually portrayed as good women trying to persuade their no-good boyfriends and husbands away from a life of crime. It seems as difficult for movie directors as for the rest of our society to consider that women may take part eagerly in criminal enterprises. Except for the occasional femme fatale, the bad guys are invariably guys.

I suspect that women are far more active in criminal subcultures than criminologists have been willing to admit. A recent flurry of work examining women in gangs, for example, has uncovered something that has been taking place for a long time: Bad girls hook up with bad boys, or other bad girls, and commit crimes. Women are arrested pawning stolen goods, working as fences, and selling drugs.

Some women hide their criminality in relationships, such as the girlfriend of a dealer, but that doesn't mean such women are innocent bystanders. A woman I once knew dealt drugs to support her own habit—cocaine. She knew what she was up to as much as any male dealer. Her parents tried to get her to give it up, paying for endless interventions and counseling sessions, but the grip of addiction was too strong.

Women who have legitimate jobs are not immune to the lure of crime. If the high figures on white-collar crime are any indication, the classic belief that women have strong inhibitions against breaking the law is doubtful. In many such crimes, such as fraud, female arrests nearly equal male.

Before Jess went off to fight in World War II, which ended his professional boxing career, he lived in Los Angeles. He tells stories about the reform school he was sent to at age twelve. There, he learned boxing, he says, and met many people who later became famous criminals. He tells the story about his zoot suit and fingertip coat, the one he still has today, and the time the police pulled him over when he was driving a stolen car—"Well," he says, "that was something."

Jess talks about growing up poor. He tells about stealing vegetables for his mother and then lying to convince her he had payed for them. He hints at a violent youth. He mentions growing up in a "tough" world, and he looks at me sideways, seeing if I understand.

He doesn't realize I grew up on the wrong side of the tracks, too. My mother drank heavily for a few years following her divorce, when I was six. Like so many in need, we used food stamps and welfare for a time, and this poverty—as well as the poverty of alcoholic neglect—still follows me. It comes out at dinner parties when I meet people who went to prep schools; it feeds a childish anger at the rich and a gnawing self-consciousness. I'm saddened to realize that Jess thinks I grew up with a wide lawn, instead of free school lunch tickets.

Perhaps more than anything, poverty influences crime and violence—for both sexes: stealing things; getting in fights, street brawls, drunken altercations; shooting off guns in bars; getting in trouble—less out of malevolence than from confusion, boredom, hopelessness, or high spirits—or getting angry, killing-mad.

"No serious student of crime or criminal justice has the slightest doubt that women, in general, just do not go in for serious crimes, especially crimes of bodily harm, of violence, of bloodshed," writes law professor Lawrence Friedman in his 1993 book *Crime and Punishment in American History*.

I find this an odd statement, because—as the figures on child abuse would indicate—women kill their children more often than men do. "In murders of their offspring, women predominated, accounting for 55% of killers," the Bureau of Justice found in a survey of family murder cases.[2]

In these murders, women do not qualify as the gentle sex. "By far the most frequent method of murder was beating: punching with fists, kicking, throwing, pushing, slapping, hitting (with belts, hammers, or wooden brushes), and striking body against furniture (shower head or walls)," the Bureau of Justice survey asserts.

The report also includes cases of children run over with cars, boiled to death, put into freezers, and disposed of in trash cans and toilets—all of which demonstrates that women do indeed "go in for" serious crimes of bodily harm and bloodshed.

Infanticide is not confined to the United States, and is not a new crime. In many societies, women have routinely murdered or maimed female babies. Chinese women once regularly killed unwanted female infants. In some African countries, the practice of performing clitorectomies is continued and maintained by women. Mothers hold their daughters down as other women cut off their clitorises with broken glass or dirty razor blades. In some cases, the entire labia is cut off and the vaginal opening is sewn up. The mortality rate for this mutilation is extremely high.

Some have questioned whether the thousands of cases

annually of sudden infant death syndrome, or SIDS, may disguise homicides by women. It can be difficult to determine if an infant died from deliberate or accidental smothering, or simply from unknown causes. In one case, landmark medical journal articles cited the deaths of five siblings as examples of SIDS. Years later, police discovered that all five children had been murdered by their mother, who suffocated them using pillows, towels, and her shoulder. She told the police she could not stand their crying.[3]

When men murder, they statistically tend to kill strangers and acquaintances, as well as family members. When women murder—and they commit about one in seven American homicides—they tend to kill family members.[4]

Women do not prey only on children. They also kill husbands. It comes as a shock to many people, but American women just about equal men in this regard.

According to the Bureau of Justice, about 40 percent of spousal murder nationwide is committed by women—a rate that fluctuates depending on ethnicity, time, and place.[5] One study on Texas homicides concluded that women in their sample were "more likely than men to resort to extreme forms of violence toward their mates."[6]

In terms of offspring and spousal murder, women truly can be as deadly as the male.

Women who commit crimes, even when their crimes are as cold-blooded as any man's, can be treated very differently by the public and the media.

The Susan Smith case is a good example of how the response to women's violence isolates the female murderer as a unique—and, in the end, an unthreatening—aberration.

It was the fall of 1994 when Smith, a twenty-three-year-old secretary at a South Carolina textile mill, claimed that an armed black man forced her out of her car at a stoplight and drove off with her two young sons, who were still in the backseat. In a period of sharp media anxiety over carjackings, the case gained instant coverage, prompting prayer vigils and television footage of Smith tearfully pleading for the return of her children.

Her story grew more colorful as the days passed. Smith claimed she begged the kidnapper to let her keep her babies. She said, "As a mother, it's only a natural instinct to protect your children from any harm."

"When a person under age twelve is murdered, a family member is the best suspect," the Bureau of Justice asserts.[7] Despite the sensationalism surrounding "milk carton children" and the now-discredited missing children movement of the early 1980s, kidnappings of children by strangers are quite rare. The probability of a child being abducted and murdered by a strange male is less than one in a million.

The police suspected Smith all along, having doubted her because of conflicting statements, badly acted grief, and an inappropriate concern over how attractive she appeared on television each night. Yet the public seemed convinced of her story about a mysterious black man who had kidnapped two white children for no apparent reason and then disappeared down a country road.

When Smith was arrested after nine days of fruitless searches, having confessed to drowning her children in a local lake, the response was outrage. People felt taken. Newspapers trumpeted that she had committed a crime "unnatural" to women. Crowds swarmed to the courthouse, screaming epithets.

The intense condemnation of Smith quickly melted away, however. A note of sympathy crept into media reports after the prosecuting attorney announced he would seek the death penalty.

We may label women who kill their children unnatural, but this doesn't always translate into harsher punishment. Jury members would later say they felt Smith was more pitiful than evil. Her lawyer described the murders as a failed suicide attempt, instead of a crime motivated by a tawdry love affair, which the evidence indicated. Suddenly, Smith went from being cast as evil incarnate to becoming an object of disgusted pity.

There may have been other factors at work here, too. In a highly publicized New York City case a year later, a drug-addicted Hispanic woman was arrested for brutally murdering her six-year-old daughter. The mother was seriously disturbed. She believed her daughter was controlled by evil spirits, and so she went about beating them out of her.

The paternalism and disbelief that marked Smith's trial was absent in this case. A minority woman from the ghetto, she represented social decay, while the middle-class white Smith elicited sympathy for her troubled background. Editorialists railed against a child-welfare system that failed to save children from such mothers. There were few calls for leniency for Awilda Lopez, the mother of Elisa Izquierdo.

The female criminal is often viewed with a sort of contemptuous sympathy, especially when she appears as conventional as a Susan Smith. The beginning of a *Psychology Today* article on women in prison advises readers they will hear stories that "tell not only of guilt, innocence, and the roots of violence, but also of healing and the beginnings of forgiveness," a sentiment that would be unthinkable for violent men.[8] One of the women interviewed beat, pistol-whipped, and, in one case, knifed her robbery victims; another took part in an infamous kidnapping in which a sixty-two-year-old businessman was starved, beaten, burned, and eventually asphyxiated to death. To me, both appeared more interested in making excuses than in finding forgiveness.

There was something about Susan Smith, with her

generic name, that struck a chord of empathy. Her face was kept devoid of makeup. She was dressed in plain, ill-fitting clothes. Her thick mousy hair was pulled back off her round face, making her look all the more vulnerable. Putting her to death seemed wrong to all but the most adamant death-penalty supporters.

The jury gave her life in prison, leaving her in a cell, as her attorney had asked for, with the ghosts of her two dead babies. As grim as that sounds, there are many men on death row who would gladly trade their sentence for her supposed haunting.

The chances of Smith being executed were slim anyhow. As of 1992, less than one and one half percent of those on death row were women, and few—if any—of these will actually be killed. Only one woman has been executed since the death penalty was resumed in 1977, compared to hundreds of men.[9]

Female crime, when exactly the same in motive, intent, and execution, is interpreted differently from male crime. It *becomes* something different. I believe if Susan Smith had been replaced by the imaginary man she accused before her confession (or by her ex-husband) the tone, the nature, the response—everything about how that case played out in the news and the community—would have changed.

Susan Smith became major news initially because of the mystery man she accused, after all, not because, like hundreds of women before and since, she murdered her children.

Women serial killers—it sounds like a contradiction.

But women multiple murderers and serial killers do exist, though they appear to be fewer in number than male serial killers.

Myra Hindley sexually tortured and killed young children

with her lover, tape-recording the victims' pleas for later enjoyment. Stella Nickell, inspired by the unsolved Tylenol murders, poisoned bottles of Excedrin, killing two. Aileen Wuornos murdered at least six men after luring them into secluded areas with promises of sex. Sylvia Seegrist is one of the unusual female multiple murderers who killed strangers in a public place. One day, she dressed up in fatigues, picked up her semiautomatic rifle, drove to the local mall, and opened fire, killing two and wounding eight. There are hundreds more.

Female multiple murderers are assumed to engage in gentler kinds of murder than men (death by poisoning, seen as a favored female method of murder, can be sadistically painful, however) and to prey only on the weak and elderly.

Some cases do fit this description. Dorothea Puente ran a boardinghouse in California and killed her boarders in order to cash their Social Security checks, then buried their corpses in her backyard. Eight bodies were found.

Women serial killers can match men in grotesquerie. Rosemary West, from Gloucester, England, is described in newspaper accounts as a "plump, nondescript figure in eyeglasses." In 1995, West was accused of the violent murders of ten people, including her own teenage daughter. Along with her husband, Fred, she was accused of sexually assaulting, torturing, and mutilating some of the victims before dismembering them and burying the body parts in their basement. Her husband hung himself in his prison cell before facing trial.

Some neighbors would later say Ms. West kept an "immaculate" family. Others would mention ringing the doorbell, only to be greeted by a stark-naked Rosemary West. By most accounts, she and her husband were mutually weird. She worked as a prostitute and brought clients home. Her husband would listen in through a baby monitor in the room.

In the coverage of women serial killers, from Wuornos to

West, what's frequently missing is the sense of horror we attach to their male counterparts. It is a Jeffrey Dahmer we fear meeting in the middle of the night, not a Rosemary West. No matter how inhuman the crime—West and Hindley, among many others, sexually torturing their victims—such women just don't seem like a threat.

Women murderers usually do not prey on female strangers, and the biggest audience for crime news is women. Crimes that titillate and scare us become big news, and whatever doesn't usually falls flat. Our lack of fear of female killers may be due in part to the mistaken belief women kill only out of self-defense, or it may be because we sense that our own lives are not threatened.

Murders of children and husbands aside, in general women don't commit as much violent crime as men. I wish I had a tidy little pet theory as to why. I don't. I think gender differences with regard to crime are probably the result of a complex mixture of socialization and social conditions—that everything from cultural messages to bias in the courts comes into play.

Boys may grow up idolizing older boys involved in gangs or leading what seem like flashy, exciting lives. Girls aren't given these criminal role models. Instead, many of us are taught to view criminal activity as fraught with danger and possible victimization. The prostitute leads a much different life from that of the pimp.

The high crime years are the teens and early twenties. During these years, girls are more likely to be held to tighter curfews and restrictions than their brothers. Later, they find their lives constricted by children.

It's interesting that the strongest adherence to standards of femininity and masculinity occurs during these high crime years. The preadolescent girl may be a tomboy and the older woman comfortable slopping around the house in old jeans, but the fifteen-year-old still obsesses over *Brides* magazine, canopy beds, Wet and Wild lipstick, and speaking in the high-pitched tones of femininity. The young man is also more stereotypically masculine than he will be for the rest of his life.

These exaggerated differences continue through the early twenties but decline once relationships and careers are in place. Older people are allowed to be much more egalitarian and androgynous.

These dramatic differences during the high crime years have persisted as women have gained equal opportunities, and this may account for at least some differences in crime.

But these are just a few elements out of many. There are numerous other factors to consider. Alcohol plays a role in many crimes, and women are still discouraged from drinking alone in taverns and other trouble spots.

There has also been a historic lack of interest in arresting women. When I worked at the county detox facility, I was initially curious as to why so few women were brought in by the police. A detox center is essentially a drunk tank—some cities allow police to hold people who are publicly intoxicated for a few hours until they sober up, without formally arresting them.

The drunk tank was housed in a building separate from the local jail and staffed by nonpolice personnel who acted as guards. We would search and check in clients, monitor their behavior, talk to them about getting treatment, and break up fights in the cells. I went from being paralyzed with fear on my first night to sincerely enjoying the job.

On a busy night, there might have been fifty or more men cursing and yelling for their lawyers, but only two or three women in their separate cell. After a while, I realized that police officers simply weren't bringing in women they found publicly intoxicated, unless the women really pushed their luck. Only when a woman was assaultive or running amok would she land in the drunk tank. I soon learned to watch these women with extra care, since they were more likely to be violent—especially to another woman. The employees were not armed, so our only defense against an attack by a client was a sort of group pig pile, along with a few holds.

In other instances, police may discourage the victims of female crime from pressing charges. A friend tells a story of how one night, angry and ashamed of the way her husband was treating her, she stormed out of a restaurant. A concerned acquaintance followed her onto the street, wanting to help. She promptly spun around and decked him, thinking he was her husband. A police officer parked at the curb saw the whole episode, but despite the fact she was adamant that the poor fellow, whose glasses were now broken and his nose bleeding, hadn't been to blame, the officer questioned him severely—and then gave *her* a ride home. When considering arrest rates, it's important to bear in mind that many women may go uncharged.

When women *are* arrested, they are less likely to be prosecuted. When prosecuted, they are less likely to be found guilty, and when found guilty, they are less likely to be sentenced to prison—and when sent to jail, they generally serve much less time.[10]

All this adds up to a legal system that ignores female crime.

In a case in my area, two skinheads—a man and a woman—were involved in an assault on a black man. The woman started it by beckoning to the victim and instigating a verbal argument. Hearing the altercation, the male skinhead appeared from nearby and punched the victim, knocking him to the ground.

Then, according to a juror from the male skinhead's trial, the woman went to work with her steel-tipped boots, viciously kicking the victim in the skull. This may explain his subsequent brain damage. But while the male skinhead was tried, convicted, and sentenced to several years for the crime, the woman skinhead was allowed to plead on lesser charges and go free—even though she appeared to be the instigator of the assault, and possibly the more serious offender.

In recent years, reform has reduced gender bias, especially in sentencing. Still, women find the courts lean in their favor. Women who murder are, on the average, given half the sentence men receive—seven years, compared with fourteen.[11] The common belief that men who kill their wives tend to get off lightly turns out to be the opposite of the truth: Women who murder their spouses generally are given a *third* the time of men.[12]

I should emphasize that this lenient treatment doesn't include minority women. The same studies that show women receive lighter sentences also indicate a strong racial bias. Black women have historically been treated far more severely by our courts than even white men.[13] Seen as tougher and more aggressive—more dangerously male— black women find presumptions of female harmlessness are suspended for them.

Once behind bars, women offenders are still treated differently. Historically, women have been viewed as a better prospect for rehabilitation. Sometimes this means more enlightened prisons, but other times it means female inmates are pushed into traditional female roles. Women prisoners still can find training limited to clerical jobs, cooking, garment manufacturing, and other traditionally feminine—and low-paying—work.

Differences in how society treats female criminals may play a role in women's lower crime rates. Like cheating at Monopoly by picking Chance cards in your favor, gender bias may reduce female crime by keeping women out of the revolving door of prison and recidivism, which traps so many male offenders. At any rate, it makes it difficult to gauge the true level of female criminality.

Criminologists have long concocted elaborate, odd, and sometimes-entertaining theories on why women commit crimes.

Cesare Lombroso, an Italian physician of the mid-1800s, studied the bones of female prisoners before concluding that women criminals have a genetic predisposition to crime, evidenced by atavistic jaws and a general ape-man appearance. Sigmund Freud believed criminal women were sexually maladjusted deviants who envied male appendages.

Many criminologists have come along since to argue that women commit crimes for just about every reason possible except those that supposedly drive men, including premenstrual syndrome, faulty chromosomes, bizarre sexual inclinations, and lesbianism.

It is men, however, who take the brunt of blame, whether through the seduction of an innocent, coercion, economic inequality, or abuse. An example is photographer Jane Evelyn Atwood. Writing for the October 5, 1994, *New York Times* op-ed page in an accompaniment to a remarkable series of photographs—women in prisons in the former Soviet Union, what was previously Czechoslovakia, New Delhi, and South Carolina—Atwood claimed that "most of the women I met said they had been provoked into committing serious crimes by the men in their lives."

According to Atwood, in one U.S. prison "almost half" of the women convicted of murder had killed husbands and boyfriends who had beaten them, and all of these said they had "repeatedly called for police help before resorting to homicide."

Atwood didn't say whether she checked out these women's stories. She seemed to assume they must have been telling the truth. But would we unquestioningly believe such stories coming from male convicts who had killed their wives or committed serious crimes?

Atwood didn't ask this question. She asked instead: "Are most women behind bars because of the men in their lives?"

The answer can be found in the research: probably not. Most female inmates have criminal records, just like men behind bars. According to a Bureau of Justice report, "Women in Prison," over two-thirds of female state prisoners had records. One in five had served time as a juvenile.

Like incarcerated men, criminal women tend to have troubled and violent backgrounds. In one study of women who killed their mates, nearly a third had records of violent crimes, such as assault and weapons charges. In over half the cases, the homicide was premeditated. Quite a few women killed husbands who were asleep, passed out, bedridden, or otherwise incapacitated. The author of the study noted that "previous arrest histories suggest that some of these offenders were neither helpless nor afraid of their victims."[14]

Some violent women may be motivated out of greed, rage, or just plain malice. Elisabeth Broderick, a wealthy divorcée who shot her ex-husband and his new wife to death in their bed, went to trial utterly unrepentant, saying the woman shouldn't have "knowingly dated a married man."[15]

Broderick gained the support of a surprising number of sympathizers. No one claimed she was abused. She was bitter her alimony was "only" sixteen thousand dollars a month.

It seems dubious to me that the more than eighteen thousand women who are arrested for motor vehicle theft each year are stealing cars to escape from abusive husbands. Or that women murder their children because their husbands "provoked" them. The explanation that women act violently only when forced into it by men remains popular, but it seldom works when applied to actual people, practices, and incidents.

Interviewing female terrorists for her book *Shoot the*

Women First, journalist Eileen MacDonald discovered women have been instrumental in many terrorist movements and groups, from the Palestinian Intifada to the Irish Republican Army. They are also sometimes directly involved in violence, including murder, bombings, and kidnappings. These women chafe considerably at the suggestion their acts are a result of coercion or blind love, taking such questions as insults to their passion for the cause.

Some feminists blame men for female crime—and some conservatives blame feminism. The idea that equality is creating a new female criminal was popularized by criminologist Freda Adler in the 1970s. Adler wrote that as "women are no longer indentured to the kitchens," they "are forcing their way into the world of major crimes."[16]

Women today do have opportunities that cloistered women of the past didn't have. Yet that doesn't mean that feminism causes crime. The women's movement has largely been in response to economic changes outside its control. If organized feminism had never happened, women today would still have to work.

Given ample opportunity, most men and women will not break taboos against acts such as murder. When people do break these taboos, as the Susan Smith case illustrates, a traditional lifestyle doesn't stop them.

A key problem with blaming feminism for crime is the assumption that women criminals are more "liberated" in their views than most women. Studies show that women in prison tend to hold traditional beliefs. Contrary to their own actions, incarcerated women will say that women should be submissive, faithful to their husbands, and not drink, smoke, or break the law.[17] In fact, both male and female prisoners tend to hold more ultraconservative values than the general population.

I find the fact that so many incarcerated women hold traditional views completely fascinating. If so many women who commit violence hold conventional beliefs, why do we continue to believe aggression is "unnatural" in women?

I believe a certain amount of female aggression *is* condoned, especially when it is posited as protecting children or the community. It was women, for instance, who spearheaded opposition to school integration and busing.

In *Warriors Don't Cry*, a memoir of one of the nine black students who integrated Little Rock Central High in 1957, Melba Pattillo Beals writes of being chased, kicked, and beaten by mobs of angry white women as she tried to attend her new school. The mobs continued their vigilance for months, and even the schoolteachers watched indifferently as the students—male and female—physically and verbally assaulted the black children.

Beals writes of one incident when her class was out in the exercise yard and three adult women protesters jumped the fence to attack her: " 'Nigger ... nigger ... ,' one woman cried, hot on my heels. 'Get the nigger.' . . . I was running at top speed when someone stuck out a foot and tripped me. I fell face forward, cutting my knee and elbow. Several girls moved closer, and for an instant I hoped they were drawing near to extend a hand and ask me if I needed help. 'The nigger is down,' one shouted. 'She's bleeding. What do you know. Niggers bleed red blood. Let's kick the nigger.' . . . As I scrambled to my feet, I looked back to see the brigade of attacking mothers within striking distance, shouting about how they weren't going to have me in school with their kids."

It was Beals's schoolmate Elizabeth Eckford who was immortalized in a photograph shown around the world. She stood there clutching her schoolbooks while surrounded by a horde of screaming, hateful women.

But because much female aggression is cast as a misguided but fundamentally well-intentioned protectionism, or as an understandable reaction to circumstances outside our control, we don't give it the same potency as male aggression. It is rarely recognized as a proactive effort designed to fulfill selfish needs; an exercise in brutality cloaked in the myth of the maternal instinct. Because of this, the most violent women can maintain women are the naturally gentler sex, and all of society will agree.

The traditional views of many violent women pose provocative questions. Will the final convincing demonstration of women's aggression be found not among those who champion equality, but, instead, among women political leaders who express violence when supporting conservative issues of family and patriotism? The feminist gains that traditionalist women might disavow have allowed them positions of power, and from podiums and political office such women may break remaining stereotypes of female passivity. You'd be hard-pressed to find a more conservative woman than Margaret Thatcher, who as prime minister led Great Britain into the war in the Falklands.

However, I don't believe the release of middle-class women from the kitchen will significantly increase violent crimes by women, any more than it will increase violent crimes by men. Breakthroughs in the glass ceiling do not drive crime. Crime tends to follow trends—from economic depressions to sentencing—that have nothing to do with women's rights. After all, the percentage of spousal murders committed by women was much the same in 1958 as it is today.[18]

Those who blame men for female crime and those who blame feminism have more in common than they think. Both associate crime and delinquency with gender. Both assume that the female criminal is more masculine than other women, either because she is forced to be or because she wants to be.

But crime is not the provenance only of men, and crime

is not necessarily masculine in intent, success, or failure. In the Bureau of Justice study on female prisoners, for instance, almost half the women said they were drunk or high on drugs when they committed the crime that landed them in jail. Like male prisoners, many reported daily drug abuse.

It's impossible to unravel these factors from socialization and biases, to know precisely what causes female crime and what inhibits it. This information gets lost in the artificial separation of the female criminal from the male.

Jess took Ernesto and me up to bouts we had scheduled in Tacoma, Washington. Several hours before the fights, we went out for Vietnamese food, and both Jess and Ernesto laughed at my judicious use of the bottle of hot-pepper oil. "You're just waving that thing for the fumes," Jess snorted, before telling us about the tacos he used to cook at a long-ago restaurant job. They sounded so good, my mouth started watering. But I found myself too shy to talk, with Ernesto sitting across from me, giving me that wise look, his arms flat across the table.

After we ate, we rambled through a small-town mall, a barnlike structure with cheap siding. We ended up in a gun store, where I read postings from survivalists while Jess and Ernesto swapped gun talk.

I felt out of place. The men I know tend to favor gun control, but they can still talk guns like they talk cars. Like many women, I know very little about guns, and my ignorance says something about female isolation from the mechanics of aggression.

The female criminal is posed as unnatural and unimportant. She is diminished, her existence denied.

On the flip side, we ascribe to men a threatening label, a power and invincibility they often don't deserve. Most crime committed by men is more likely to take the form of a barroom fight than a malevolent assault on a total stranger.

Neither cartoonish depiction of the sexes is accurate. And for women, neither is very healthy. We end up fearing men as we diminish our own ability to defend ourselves from them. Our one-sided assumptions of aggression forget that women can—and need to be able to—fight back.

Eight ✦

THE POWER OF FEAR

There are posters on the gym walls, which Jess pointed out one day. They are of his best-known fighter, Adofo Akil, when his name was still Mike Colbert. He fought against Marvelous Marvin Hagler for the middleweight title. Colbert, who now sits on the Oregon Boxing Commission, still shows up at local amateur fights.

When Jess tells the story about Colbert's title shot against Hagler, he laughs and shakes his head. Colbert was ahead on the cards when, at the end of the eleventh round—some say after the bell rang—Hagler broke his jaw.

Colbert could have stopped the fight because of the injury, and perhaps won it on a technical foul. But instead, he returned to his corner, kept quiet about the injury, and went back out in the twelfth round to continue fighting.

All Hagler had to do was watch for his chance. He broke the other side. Jess says you could just see the hinges of Colbert's jaw fall open and the blood gush out. He went down like a sack of potatoes, and Jess says it took awhile before he forgave his boxer for risking a career-ending injury.

But he tells the story with secret pride. Colbert had heart.

Kill the Body, the Head Will Fall

* * * *

The image of the boxer rising to meet his opponent again, injured and racked with pain, invigorates as it repels. I can see all too vividly the broken hinges of Colbert's jaw. It amazes me how he continued to fight while experiencing such pain.

How little fear he must have had. Or how well he mastered his fear. What heart he had, to fight back.

For a lot of women, the idea of fighting back when injured, to walk into your opponent's blows knowing you will get hurt, is foreign, nearly unimaginable.

Ours is a society that makes it hard for women to defend themselves. The same socialization that may make us less likely to commit crime also appears to make us more fearful—in negative, debilitating ways.

In the course of researching this book, whenever I told someone its subject was women and aggression, the person invariably thought I meant women as victims.

But most crime victims are men, preyed upon by other men. Over three times as many men as women are murdered every year, and thousands more are victimized in muggings, shootings, robberies, and assaults.

In fact, women and the elderly are the two groups least likely to be victimized by crime. If you are a white woman over the age of sixty, you win the bonus prize: Your chances of being the victim of a violent crime are substantially less than just about everyone else's. Yet it is women and the elderly who fear crime the most, a situation some have termed "the paradox of fear."[1]

Professor Mark Warr is an expert on the subject of fear and crime, and he has published groundbreaking studies on the subject. I called him at the University of Texas at Austin, where he teaches sociology.

Warr told me he has found that in general people's fear corresponds closely to the likelihood of victimization. Logically enough, the most feared crime is one of the more common: residential burglary. In keeping with its low rate of occurrence, murder falls below "having strangers loiter near your home late at night" and "being hit by a drunk driver while driving your car."

But there is one crime in which fear is all out of proportion to the likelihood of victimization. That crime is rape, and those who fear it most, of course, are women. Rape, according to Warr, is "currently a central fear in the lives of a large proportion of women."

The Bureau of Justice reports that roughly two out of every thousand women are victims of a sexual assault each year. This includes rapes, attempted rapes, and other sex crimes.[2] Since the Bureau of Justice arrives at its numbers through a national survey that includes unreported crimes, many experts consider this a fair estimate. Others think it is too low.

It would be interesting to know if women's intense fear is a recent trend, but the study of fear itself is relatively new. One study by another set of researchers did find that men also feared sexual assault, presumably by other men, though not to the same degree as women.[3]

Rape is a crime with a special threat. Women in Warr's surveys rated rape with injuries ("A man forcibly rapes a woman. Her injuries require hospitalization.") as a more serious crime than women murdering their husbands without any given provocation ("A woman stabs her husband. As a result, he dies.").[4]

Fear of rape constricts women's behavior in dramatic ways. Nearly half of the women in Warr's studies avoided going out alone and going out at night, compared to less than 10 percent of the men. Warr notes that "a little risk goes a long way in producing fear" of rape. There is a sense of vulnerability operating here that doesn't exist for muggings or beatings.

I know women who won't open the door to a stranger, even in the daytime. Their fear has literally driven them indoors. And there, they double-check locks at night, toss and turn when husbands are out of town, and jump out of their skins at the slightest noise. I'm the first to admit that there are times I can barely sleep when alone in the house.

"Then again, I'm tired of feeling as though evil is lurking around every corner, stalking me like a psycho killer. Fear is enervating, paranoia debilitating," journalist Lucy Kaylin wrote in a first-person account of her fears in the January 1992 *Mademoiselle*. Kaylin described an existence controlled by "living in perpetual anticipation of life's horrors," a threat to personal safety that "seems worst for women."

Her fear is sharp and intense, and, like many women, she finds little comfort in being physically fit or being aware of her surroundings. The fear she finds so enervating is real, though largely unfounded. Danger doesn't stalk women more than it does men. Fear does.

Society encourages this fear in women. While some would point to men as the cause—thinking they must be hugely brutal to inspire this tremendous fear (and leading to the conclusion that there must be a massive number of unreported rapes)—I think we overlook women's role. Mothers impose protective measures on their daughters. Women's magazines inflame this fear with sensational journalism.

Our culture exploits this fear. Sitcoms and movies depict the woman who would walk to her car at night as an endangered fool. In the lurid movie scenes of rape, women who try to fight back do so pathetically, hitting with frantic little paws. Rarely is a woman depicted as successfully defending herself against an attacker.

Violation seems to have special meaning to women not just because it may happen but because women are taught there is nothing they can do about it.

For all the attention paid to women's alleged vulnerability to rape, few girls are taught how to defend themselves physically. Self-defense training is not nearly as widespread as the fear of victimization would lead you to think. Myths about women's physical weakness and nonaggressive nature have us convinced that women are unable to fight back. Self-defense courses are frequently inadequate. You just can't expect to make up for a lifetime of physical self-doubt with a two-hour class.

Self-defense requires proactive aggression. Colbert rose after the bell with a broken jaw, and he crossed that ring to face Hagler, knowing he would get hit again, knowing it would cause unbearable pain. Men who would never willingly face such pain can still imagine themselves doing so, and they carry themselves as if they would, but women are seldom granted this potential. Because we cannot imagine ourselves fighting back—and honestly believe we are unable to—we can't. What's more, everyone else knows it.

The constraints women impose on their lives may, in the paradox of fear, account for their lower rates of victimization: Women don't put themselves at risk. By not walking alone at night or taking other chances, women may be protecting themselves from crime that men, naïvely convinced of a safety that doesn't exist, walk right into. According to Warr, this is pure conjecture at this point. More research needs to be done.

Even if true, we may want to assess the negative results of this excessive, unreasonable fear. As Kaylin writes, fear can be enervating, paranoia debilitating. It rarely gives us strength.

If the denial of female aggression has contributed to women's unreasonable fear (that we can't protect ourselves), what does such fear mean not just for women but also for our families and communities?

Surely women's fear has effects beyond obsessively checking locked doors at night.

When we tear apart our childrens' Halloween candy looking for razor blades, for example, we are conveying a distrust in the world born out of a disproportionate fear. Lack of documented cases of actual trick-or-treat candy tampering suggests this fear is more a result of urban myth than a real threat.[5] When we needlessly fear that husbands, coworkers, and other trusted men might someday assault us, we allow irrational fears to intrude into our relationships and our daily lives.

And when our fear turns to anger, it can be devastating.

Fear isn't harmless. Professor Warr points out one of the outcomes of such distrust is attacks on individual liberties.

The irony of fear, which men as well as women display, is that it can make people who feel *privately* vulnerable act *socially* aggressive.

Fear of crime seems to create a sense of social panic—a sense that time is limited and running out. Preventive measures won't do. The answer has to be immediate, swift, and harsh. Lynne Abraham, a prosecutor in Philadelphia who is famous for seeking the death penalty, asserts: "We are so overwhelmed by cruelty and barbarism, and most people feel the legal system doesn't work. We feel our lives are not in our own hands. . . . All of our cases now are multiple gunshot executions, houses set on fire and six children burned to death. This is Bosnia."[6]

But this isn't Bosnia. Snipers don't lurk outside our office doors. Soldiers don't rampage through our cities. Bombs do not drop on our streets. The horror of gunshot cases and children dying in house fires doesn't mean our society is comparable to the pervasive violence of a civil war. With minor bumps and dips, violent crime has stayed steady for decades, for both male and female offenders.[7]

The mood of vulnerability that Abraham cites—the sense that the individual is overwhelmed by cruelty and barbarism—endorses a collective violence. The woman who feels she cannot fight back by herself groups with her friends, engages the men, and becomes actively aggressive. As the traditionalism of many incarcerated women suggests, she may endorse vigilantism, call for the caning of wayward students, or demand the castration of sex offenders. From her position of supposed vulnerability, she wields an incredible amount of power.

Of course, men act socially aggressive as well, but women's heightened sense of fear would seem to have an additional impact: an added drive to circle the wagons. In this manner, the modern women's movement's emphasis on victimization may have had the inadvertent effect of popularizing conservative anticrime efforts, thus setting the stage for class and ethnic hostility.

Clearly, women's fear of crime—synonymous with rape—has been a major foundation of racism. Women in the South used to incite lynch mobs with false allegations of rape, eagerly provide the fuel for the execution pyre, and cheer on the killings. (An estimated four to five thousand men were victims of lynching.) Women who had accused black men of sex crimes would occasionally be given the honor of being the first to riddle their corpses with bullets, a common lynching custom.[8]

Rather than simply being the excuse for racial violence that some assume, women were often the instigators of it. While most accounts portray the Ku Klux Klan as an almost exclusively male organization, Klanswomen of the 1920s were "responsible for some of its most vicious, destructive results," according to historian Kathleen Blee. The real power of the KKK was not in night riding and other male activities, which were visible but sporadic, but in its far-reaching economic and political control. It was women who organized the devastating boycotts of Jewish stores, the efforts to rid schools of Catholic teachers, and it was women who dedicated untold hours to creating a massive, nearly perfect political machine—all from the knitting-circle atmosphere of their "klaverns." Klanswomen normalized bigotry, bringing it into churches and homes.[9]

Women playing upon the fear of crime is by no means confined to the past, and by no means confined to women on the far right. From politicians to advocacy groups, many treat women's fear as a commodity, to be manipulated into votes, funds, public outrage.

Where does women's fear lead? Such a strong emotion must have an ongoing effect, like a subterranean stream, undercutting so much in our lives.

Beliefs that women are not aggressive do not create a more passive, beautiful world. They create the debilitating fear journalist Kaylin describes. They can make women retreat and then lash out. They may turn us into the kind of people we are not supposed to be: angry, judgmental, aggressively afraid.

Rather than making us more violent, maybe recognizing female aggression can help women to enjoy the same responsibilities—and to take the same risks—that men do.

Aggression does not exist in a sphere by itself. It exists in the context of relationships, among friends, family, and foes; it is created amidst personal desires and emotions. Any boxer might tell of warmth in the middle of violence, a community where aggression is entwined with human need.

Nine ⟶

JESS

In her book *On Boxing*, Joyce Carol Oates writes that a boxer is his body. The condition of the muscles, the strength of the heart, the weight class and stamina—all define the boxer. A fighter in good condition may enter the ring with a bad flu—the kind that would put most people in bed for a week—and fight his way through ten or twelve hard rounds. He will be sickly with sweat and his chest flushed, but his body, trained beyond a point of fitness to something akin to remembrance, will go on.

The fighter is his body in the most intrinsic way: the length of the limbs, the shape of the tendons. In professional fights, the fighter will be weighed and his arm span measured. His arms are spread out like the wings of a bird, and the span is measured from the tip of the fingers on one hand to the tip of the other hand, across the shoulders. It is called the reach, and whoever has the longer presumably has the advantage. But it matters, too, how loose the fighter is: if he can roll the shoulder forward into the punch, extending his reach forward.

A fighter can hone his muscles, but he is also his reflexes. The reflexes are one of the first things to go in an older boxer. You can see it in the comeback fighters: the look of strain, puzzlement at a body that once worked perfectly but is now balking, growing dull. By the time the fighter sees the opening to throw a right, it's lost. By the time he sees the punch coming and moves to slip it, it's too late.

"I used to have speed and finesse and used to never get hit," Larry Holmes, former heavyweight champ, said following a ponderous, painful bout against a fighter he could easily have demolished in earlier days. "Now I'm flat-footed and take a shot here and take a shot there."[1]

In the younger fighter, the reflexes are sharp, the hands capable of moving at a blur. The body is something to be molded and used, a tool capable of taking punishment. Most people don't understand how resilient the human body is, how many times one can be hit and go on; how resilient the internal organs are, to take deep-driven blows, how thick the skull.

But one day, as much from time as punishment, the body simply gives up. Before his ninety-eighth fight defending his superlightweight title against the beautiful David Kamau, Julio Cesar Chavez complained of his back hurting, his hands hurting, his body being deeply tired. Chavez won the fight on points, but I thought he looked slow, desperate. At thirty-three, he was racing the clock to meet his goal of a hundred professional victories before retirement. Chavez is—was—one of the finest body punchers.

In the older fighter, the body becomes disobedient. It fails.

For the fighter, this failure of the body signals the end of a career—sometimes a career that can be almost tragic because of pitfalls, lack of title opportunities, a prize held tantalizingly out of reach. Such as Joe Hipp, the Native American fighter from the West Coast. Hipp is a natural heavyweight who has always carried a spare tire around his middle, a big, smooth, hard belly, an egg-shaped frame.

Hipp's professional career has survived knee surgery, fractured hands, broken bones, weight problems, and all the other failings of his body, and each time he has recovered to return to the ring. Now he faces the one failing that no fighter recovers from: age.

Age has always been a part of this sport, recognized and debated. When is a fighter too old? Is it better to retire or to go down fighting?

Boxing is the sport of the very young. By the time they reach their early thirties, most fighters find their careers are in decline. The fact that I am a woman makes this point irrelevant, anyway, since I can't really go anyplace.

There are women professionals out there who might disagree. They would point to championship women's tournaments held in other countries, fights here in the United States, purses that might go as high as a few thousand dollars. Women boxers occasionally appear on *Fight Night at the Forum,* or the USA network's *Tuesday Night Fights,* with the ever-enjoyable commentary by former lightweight champ Sean O'Grady. Christy Martin and Deirdre Gogarty stole the show from Mike Tyson on a March 1996 card, advancing female boxing several years in just six rounds.

At the time of this writing, the international Olympic committee is considering allowing women's boxing (though women can fight as amateurs, so far we have not been allowed in the Olympics), another major step forward.

There are quite a few women professionals from England, Canada, and other countries. These women are dedicated, considering how little money is involved. But lack of money is one reason why so few women are able to pursue boxing full-time.

I have wondered at times why Jess devotes time to me. He knows I will never win him the acclaim that rewards a coach, though he does seem proud of my progress. I watch him devote time to many fighters who are clearly not going anyplace, either. He trains older men who just want to get in shape, younger men who haven't the time or dedication to compete, and now other women as well.

Like many boxing coaches, Jess trains fighters because that is what he does. He has grown too old for competition. Retired, a fighter can always stay in the game by managing, promoting, and especially by coaching.

The history of boxing is really more a history of trainers than of their fighters. The fighters themselves may become famous, but their moments of ascendancy are brief. It is the legendary trainers—Cus D'Amato, Angelo Dundee—who stay with us, who mold body after body, fighter after fighter.

Since my first day at the gym, I have been aware of Jess's age. He is past seventy, and although he is energetic, there is no denying he is elderly and somewhat infirm. As the months go by, medical problems crop up. He had to have an operation on his foot—complications, I think, from adult-onset diabetes. I visited him in the hospital wearing a pink flowered dress he exclaimed over. He had never seen me in a dress before. As we talked, Jess held old fight magazines in his trembling hands. Some of his other fighters went to visit him. I wasn't the only one.

Months later, it was as if Jess had suddenly disappeared from the gym. He was there one day, giving orders, buckling helmets, joking with me as I prepared to leave. I said good-bye, then drove home in the summer heat, and then the next day he didn't show at all, or the next. I asked other fighters, other coaches, but no one seemed to know where he was. "Maybe he's sick," someone said.

I was aware of a worry that surprised me. Our relationship had evolved slowly over the months, almost sneaking up on me. I tried to contact him—I have his home phone number and he has mine. The news was bad. Jess had had a mild stroke.

He was in the hospital only a few days. One of his hands, already spotted and easily injured because of blood thinning caused by aspirin medication, was now as soft and quiet as a dead baby.

I found myself startlingly close to tears. I had never had a relationship like this before. Not because I grew up father-less, which I did, but because with Jess the rules on age and intimacy are confused. Our relationship is not the relationship of a father and a daughter. It is not that committed, not that formal. Nor is it the relationship, strictly, of a coach and his fighter, because I am a woman. That changes things. Where do an old fighter and a grown woman, unrelated, fit into our classifications of relationships? There isn't a name for it.

As soon as he could, Jess returned to the gym. Others had to help him put the helmets on, buckle straps, tie the gloves. He was shaky, weak. His hand slowly came back to life, and he could move the fingers a little. He showed me how he tries to make a fist, and I was terrified at the sight of that hand, helpless in its struggle.

I said nothing to the other trainers, since Jess didn't want them to know. He told some of his fighters, and I think the word got out, but Jess mistrusts the motives of some of the people in the local fight world, and he seemed to fear how they will use this information.

He was trained as a fighter. He didn't want to seem vul-nerable. I think he still sees his opponents looking for weak-nesses, for a body that is failing—more than his opponents, the world at large—studying him for the time to deliver a final blow.

Ten ✒

WOMEN IN
THE MILITARY

Sometimes sparring comes infrequently. One summer, the gym was nearly empty, tranquil.

Other times, sparring can occur often, like a gift. For a few weeks, I was able to work with Miguel, a fighter preparing to turn pro. Miguel weighs about 130 pounds and has a solid, muscled frame.

The more I get into the ring, the more I feel at ease and eager for more. Slowly, I lose my fear. It makes me exultant. At the same time, constancy blurs sparring, making it common. Time after time, I crawl through those ropes; time after time, I face a partner and touch gloves. Time after time, the bell rings, until I feel the emotional importance of all that is happening is becoming ordinary—although never deadened by frequency.

Each day is magically different, because the same opponent can change dramatically round to round, minute to minute. And at the same time, you are changing, with practice and training. It explains why the public so often wants to believe there is a fix when a boxer once beaten badly triumphs, or when one once unbeatable is sent to the canvas.

Kill the Body, the Head Will Fall

The eccentricities of the human body, and the human spirit, are encapsulated in boxing. The opponent you face right now, in this ring, is never the same as he was the month or day—or even the moment—before.

This is a truly frightening thing about boxing. It can be so accidental. Whether you win or lose sometimes has as much to do with pure chance as with training: a slip a referee counts as a knockdown; a bad case of nerves; a bad case of judges. No matter how hard you train, part of you places your hope not in your strengths but in your opponent's weaknesses, and also on whatever charm or religion you may have, because there is never a guarantee.

I learned this with Miguel, the way we surprised each other. Boxers learn one another's styles. You discover if they have a strong jab or devastating body punches, as Miguel does. He learned I like to come in full-bore, but at the same time I still forget to tuck my chin in, making myself vulnerable. But no matter how much you learn, the opponent will always be unpredictable. A tiny change in stance, a lateral movement here, an uppercut there—each can change the entire tone of a fight.

One day, sparring with Miguel was like hot wires downed by a storm. I got in the ring and a packed gym found reason to crowd around. A sense of anticipation filled the air, though I didn't know why—Miguel and I had been sparring together often. It may have had to do with several new fighters in the gym. They gawked at me: a woman. I was wearing my new headgear and gloves, which Jess had finally talked me into buying. They are Reyes, a popular brand. Both helmet and gloves are candy apple red leather, the headgear light and cushiony over my skull, leaving my face open, the gloves Mexican-style, which means less padding over the knuckles and a heavier, firmer wrist, which Jess laced tightly on my arms.

Miguel had just finished two rounds with another fighter,

116

and as I climbed through the ropes, I wondered if he would be tired. When the bell rang, however, there was a sudden explosion. Jess and Chuck snorted and laughed at the side of the ring, as suddenly, with the final sound of that bell ringing across the gym, Miguel and I were at each other's throats, feathers fluttering to the ground.

I didn't plan on that coming, and I didn't have time to figure it out.

Everything was a blur of action. Miguel cornered me and threw a beautiful combination—a set of blows to the body, and then suddenly that crushing left hook to the chin. I wondered if I threw anything before—you can never quite remember who threw the first punch—but that doesn't matter, because I was on top of him, he was on top of me, and the fight was on.

We raced around the ring, cutting each other off, squaring off, and throwing hard, fast punches. Not a second was spared—not a moment passed when we considered, or reconsidered—just these fast combinations, constant and unrelenting.

The round was going by faster and faster. Jess was giving advice to Miguel. Chuck was talking to me. "Where is your jab?" he asked. And I responded by moving quickly left to right, forking that puppy out and tapping Miguel in the face with it, keeping him off. Miguel only bored in tight and unleashed body shots. He drove me against the ropes and I dipped slightly, using my forearms to block the blows as I bobbed and weaved, then came back swinging. My hands were talking before I could tell them what to do, and I threw a blurringly fast combination: a right to the body, a series of left hooks to the head, followed by a chopping straight right to the chin. Miguel was dazed, backed off quickly.

The crowd around the gym made a little sound of appreciation. A few of the boys laughed, an exuberant sound. Miguel responded. I responded. We didn't stop. I was throw-

ing furiously to his dipping, bobbing head—angry, I let go—
and the bell suddenly rang.

We stopped, smashed gloves. Jess and Chuck warned me
not to stand up so straight, to keep my chin down. Chuck
popped out my mouthpiece and rinsed it and my mouth
with a strong spray of warm water from a bottle, then pushed
the mouthpiece back in.

The next round started.

It was almost as furious, and twice as fast. Miguel, now on
his fourth round of sparring, was in full flower. He drove,
bobbed, and weaved. I could sense strength in his body.
When we got in close, he pushed. From the side of the ring,
Chuck said, "I know he's stronger than you, but push back."
I tried, but my strength was slipping. He was bigger, and
stronger. He kept driving at me with those body punches,
and I was open for them: hard, punishing shots.

Punches to the head don't really hurt—at least in a sharp,
painful sense—but blows to the body can take the starch
out of you. Getting hit in the midsection sends the most
horrible paralyzing, burning sensation up and down you
before it turns your legs rubbery and soft. Every fighter
knows that if you want to take out your opponent, go to the
body.

Jess stopped me suddenly. He signaled me to the side of
the ring, told me to duck in with Miguel, to work on the
inside, punching close in. I was standing too erect again,
which is why I was getting hit easily. Miguel and I touched
gloves and began fighting once more, midway into the
round. The action was so fast, the sweat was already pouring
down me. I dropped to drive a straight right into his stomach, right above the waistband of his trunks, then returned
to the head. He didn't wilt under my pressure, but returned.
In close, in the middle of the ring, he chanted under his
breath, "*come on, come on.*" I could hear him, feel the hot
powdery scent of his breath on my cheek. But my hands at

this point were dulling; my reflexes were off because of those body blows.

I summoned the energy to strike back. Miguel drove me into a corner with a sharp jab, cut me off. It was the corner where Jess, Chuck, and some of the fighters stood nearby. I could feel the spongy rubber of the corner mat behind my back. Miguel began really unleashing his strength. One body punch sunk in so deeply, right under my rib cage— over the liver—that I let out this half-involuntary grunt: *uuummph*.

The sound, as soft as it is, was caught in the air. Everyone heard it.

Miguel instantly apologized, under his breath. Before I could even think about it, I used the opportunity to dodge out of the corner and send a straight left his way. I was laughing. His chin crumpled. Of course he returned the favor. The moment passed, and we were shifting, tired but still as fast, across the ring.

Later, after the sparring session, Jess pointed to my midsection. He was worried about the body shots I took. I tried to make a joke out of it, saying that *that* should teach me about defense. I know he doesn't worry with the guys. It's my internal female organs that concern him. I said that Miguel throws a good punch to the belly. Jess looked pleased at this compliment to Miguel, but he was still disquieted by worries about my midsection, the land of strange female parts.

Miguel, who was standing nearby, suddenly dashed off. I worried instantly that he felt ill at ease with me and upset.

I was suddenly struck by how discordant I can feel, here in this gym full of male fighters. There are times when I feel accepted, and this acceptance is genuine, and yet there are other times when my presence is as painful and sharp as a knife.

I know how disruptive I am in this gym. I know the disruption is like a deep fault that keeps the splintered parts of Jess's team from forming into a whole.

I know I am the girl whom the boys have to fight.

Women fighting men. What is a strong taboo actually has a long history, from Queen Boadicea, the Celtic leader who took her troops against the Romans, to the esteemed pilot Rufina Gasheva, a hero of the Soviet Union who flew 850 missions in World War II.

Their lives have been largely glossed over, and lost, but women have been involved in militaries and revolutions since before recorded history.

Sometimes we have been directly involved in fighting. It was a nearly all-female mob of thousands that stormed Versailles in 1789, looting and murdering in revolutionary anger. In India, lower-caste hero Phoolan Devi was the female leader of an all-male revolutionary gang that killed at least twenty during the early 1980s. In Zimbabwe, Parliament member Margaret Dongo was one of many women guerrilla warriors who fought to overthrow the white government; today, she is still as feared as she is respected.

Other times, our role has been peripheral, or behind the lines: the women of Nazi Germany who sent Hitler adoring love letters; the nurses and technicians of American wars. Women have shown themselves to be capable of the fiercest warmongering, and they are generally just as supportive of war efforts as men.

It's only been in the past few decades, as women have moved from the rear of the battlefield toward the front—and, importantly, from taking orders to giving them—that our role in war has suddenly ignited intense controversy.

The female soldier confronts society with an aggression as real and as controlled as a man's. She is not hysterical, a fishwife, an irrational shrew. She is calm and confident. She causes deep discomfort not just because she is aggressive but also because she breaks the rules against combat between the sexes.

The 1991 Gulf War woke America to women's role in the military. Over 41,000 women served. Fourteen died.

Never before had so many women fought in an American war. Overwrought articles on the "mommie war" appeared, complete with photos of military mothers kissing their babies good-bye. As usual, pollsters raced to capture what the public made of all this.

But just as the Gulf War demonstrated a positive move toward allowing women the same opportunities as men, it also brought old fears tumbling out of the closet. Some worried that the women wouldn't be able to stand up to the job physically. Others fretted that the troops would engage in sexual shenanigans, or that women would be captured by the enemy and raped. A lot of people couldn't quite figure out just *what* women were doing over there. What was the difference, they asked, between direct and indirect combat, and why were women dying if prohibited from the former?

Politicians convened hearings and created commissions to discuss women in combat. What started with gravity reverted to exclamation points. The opposition was reduced to alarmism. They were puzzled as to why the country didn't balk when women started coming home in body bags. Instead, the families mourned privately, for sons and daughters alike. No one could figure out the mood of the country, if there ever is one mood.

The polls came back. Most Americans now support women being allowed into at least some areas of direct combat.

"I would take the ten best," Capt. Chris Lemay with the Canadian Forces Office of Public Affairs answers. I have asked him who he would rather have under his command, men or women. "It's not a matter of gender," Lemay says, "but a matter of who's the best person for the job."

Lemay speaks with a strong French-Canadian accent, a heady mixture of lilting vowels and thick English. He seems intent to convince me that the 1989 ruling allowing Canadian women into all combat posts—including the infantry, armor, and artillery—has been successful. But his eagerness to persuade does not seem like the hand-wringing of an administrator hiding faults as much as it does a commander speaking from a deep affection for his troops.

Lemay has trained these new women combat soldiers. His firsthand experience has convinced him that women are capable of the punishing life of a foot soldier.

In the United States, women are still barred from direct-combat posts in the infantry, armor, and field artillery units. More combat positions, such as fighter pilots and some artillery positions, are being opened to women. But the major routes for advancement are in the small percentage of posts that remain closed.

Several lessons from Canada are now clear. Some women are physically capable of being foot soldiers. Others are not—and neither are all men. Lemay points out that quite a few men are physically weak and unfit.

During the first few years combat posts were opened, Canadian women did well in artillery and armor, but many failed infantry training. Part of the reason is that large numbers of women were recruited, and not many had an idea of what they were getting into.

Now less women try out for the posts, but those who do seem better prepared. In 1994–1995, for example, only five women tried for Canada's small infantry force, compared with 672 men. Three of the women graduated, making the female success rate 60 percent. Comparatively, 82 percent of the men made it. In artillery, four women entered the course and three of them graduated, for a 75 percent success rate, compared with a 96 percent success rate for men. Only one woman trained as an infantry officer, and she passed.[1]

These numbers are too small to be used to draw conclusions about attrition rates. Just a few additional women each year could raise or lower the success rates dramatically. It's obvious, however, that of those women interested in combat, enough are capable of meeting the requirements to allow them to try.

Lemay dismisses the oft-heard concern that standards have been lowered to make room for women. "The standards are set by what's needed in the field," he says. "It's not an issue to say, 'The standards are set for the guys or for the women.' . . . In armor and artillery, for example, they have to be able to lift these heavy shells." He hasn't found women's presence hurts troop cohesion or damages military effectiveness.

Near the end of our interview, Lemay mentions with pride that one of his women infantry soldiers was serving with the United Nation's forces in Bosnia. Put to the test, women prove they, too, can go successfully to battle.

Technology has changed the face of war. As the United States found in Iraq, there are no solid front lines anymore. Combat can mean manning advanced weaponry far from the enemy or firing from offshore. It also can mean that women supposedly prohibited from direct combat end up under long-range enemy fire, which is how women died in the Gulf. Army captain Mimi Finch says that modern battle is "much more confused. Everyone is at risk."[2]

Because of these advances, combat policies that sound workable on paper are somewhat inane in practice. Retired Maj. Gen. Jeanne Holm points out in her book *Women in the Military* that women in the Gulf were allowed to serve on tactical air bases targeted by Iraqi Scud missile attacks but were banned from better-protected aircraft carriers offshore. They were shot down while flying supply helicopters but were barred from piloting combat aircraft.

Combat policies tend to be driven more by politics and moral concerns than by objective research. Put a man and a woman in a trench together and supposedly you'll have trouble.

There have been some problems with sexual relationships in the military. Thirty-six women got pregnant on one American ship during the Gulf War, leading some to call it the "Love Boat," signaling a dire need for leadership and control, or at least birth control. This ship was unusual, though.

Sexual relationships developed in the armed forces when women were confined to supportive posts such as secretaries, and they will continue to develop regardless of whether women are allowed equal opportunities. The question is whether such relationships endanger the forces, and so far the answer is no.

The Love Boat aside, pregnancy did not turn out to be a hindrance in the Gulf War. Even when pregnancies are included, men tend to miss more days on duty than do women, due to sports injuries, alcohol abuse, and disciplinary causes.

A 1995 navy policy shows that the inevitable pregnancies that come with a co-ed volunteer force seem best addressed by a reasonable policy. The policy gives pregnant soldiers full natal care, and returns them to their former or equivalent duties without professional downgrading. Pregnancy, the navy concluded, does not seem to be having any effect on military readiness.[3]

Despite House Speaker Newt Gingrich's comment that women soldiers are prone to "infections" every thirty days, menstrual periods also do not create the hindrance some worry over. As English journalist Kate Muir discusses in her book *Arms and the Woman*, women in the Gulf found that menstrual periods turned out to be minor annoyances at most. Muir spent days in the field with women soldiers, and she writes eloquently about the heat and discomfort of the battlefield, where "soldiers of either sex hated the dust storms, the stinking chemical latrines, the constant stress of Scud attacks and the boiling hot, charcoal-lined, chemical warfare suits that turned their skin black. . . . 'the separate toilets and shower problems' also dissipated in the desert, when creating a ladies meant no more than digging an extra hole in the sand. . . ."[4]

Yet another fear also dissipated in the desert of the Persian Gulf—the fear that the sexual assault of women prisoners of war would damage troop morale. Incidents of women POWs being sexually assaulted are uncommon. A woman flight surgeon was sexually molested after her helicopter was downed in Iraq. She later stood before a presidential commission to assert that while the assault was unpleasant, it was also an "occupational hazard" of war.[5] It was clear she did not want her trauma to be used against other women.

In all the papers, reports, and military documents I've read that concern themselves with the rape of women POWs, few deal with male sexual victimization. There are cases of male soldiers being sodomized and assaulted, by the enemy and their comrades, but such incidents appear seldom reported by the victims, and when they are, they get little attention. During the time the Tailhook sexual harassment scandal was front-page news, for instance, two different cases of American male sailors raping other male sailors came to light.[6]

When examining the arguments marshaled by critics of women in combat, it's easy to lose sight of what is happening within the forces themselves. Looking into this topic, I initially found soldiers like Chris Lemay surprising. The last thing I had expected to hear from a male officer was his spirited praise of women combat soldiers.

Like so many women, my opinion of the armed forces has been shaped by highly publicized stories, such as Shannon Faulkner's rough treatment at the hands of the Citadel, the private all-male military school she fought for years to enter but soon left, exhausted and despairing.

I was pulling for Faulkner. I admired what the Mexican guys refer to as *cojones*. And I felt for her when she dropped out. The attack from other women was merciless. Women columnists—many not exactly svelte themselves—criticized her weight and savaged her appearance. How many of us could cope with such pressure and publicity, and at that young age? And how could the commanders at the Citadel be so obtuse not to recognize this young woman's incredible courage? You would think they would welcome such a fighting spirit with open arms.

The Citadel, like Tailhook, is the kind of story that makes the news. But it does not reflect the attitudes of the military as a whole. At the same time Faulkner left the Citadel, in August of 1995, a record sixty-five women quietly took their places in Norwich University's military college, which has admitted women since the early 1970s.[7]

Most military academies accept women, and new zero-tolerance policies are making headway fighting sexual harassment. The Undersecretary of Defense for Personnel and Readiness, Edwin Dorn, believes that as women "begin to occupy more of the war-fighting roles" and so achieve leadership positions, sexual harassment will decline just as racial harassment did following the integration of the forces.[8]

While there is still a great deal of sexism in the military, there are many commanders who are genuinely committed to equality. Curiously, it is the military's functional approach to aggression that allows this. Having seen that women can perform, some officers waste no time changing their mind about allowing them to. It is those distanced from the field who remain most ensconced in sexism.

It is pragmatism, rather than the pie-in-the-sky idealism some politicians claim, that drives efforts to open all military posts to women. Rear Adm. Philip Quast, Assistant Chief of Naval Operations, asserts that the policies against women in combat are actually hurting the navy. "I have personally seen mixed-gender ships turned around, broken off from an engagement or an evolution simply because they were reaching an invisible line that, if they crossed it, would put them into a combat zone," he said. "These lines are artificialities. They are counterproductive, they are wasteful and, frankly, they are dumb."[9]

The issue of effectiveness is a good one. At the same time the percentage of women increases in the armed forces, technological advances demand specialized training. Removing a female specialist from a ship or troop when fighting breaks out has the potential to undermine the forces.

Policies against allowing women into combat worked in the past, when men were drafted into the armed forces and when technological skills were less crucial. Today, these policies are no longer functional. The military has recognized that women are a better "buy," with the average female recruit better educated than her male peers. This is why we so often see commercials for the army appealing directly to women. In an all-volunteer force, women have not just become indispensable; they've become highly desirable.

Women continue to find themselves cut out of good-paying career paths because of the combat policies that remain. This is not a minor issue: Over 28,000 American women enlist in the armed forces every year. It is especially pertinent to black women, who are now one out of every fourteen army sergeants, and who have found in the armed services a solid career often not available to them in civilian life.[10]

But there is also a symbolic loss. Combat is the reason we have armed forces. It is the point of soldiers, their identity. Whether we endorse that or not, allowing men to develop this identity but refusing it to women has meaning for our society far beyond war and conflict.

Even when she is in reality near the front of the battlefield, facing danger and taking responsibility equally with men, the woman soldier is symbolically relegated to the rear. No matter how you try to get around it, the perception remains that her skills are inferior.

The female soldier puts us face-to-face with the fact that women can fight—not just in passion or anger but for a cause—or for the excitement of combat, the personal challenge of pitting oneself against another. What's more, they want to, thousands upon thousands of them.

Women's military service is one of the more frank examples of women's aggression. Most will not relish violence, although some will take joy in it. But all find in themselves a capacity to compete—against men and against one another.

Eleven ⟶

FEMALE COMPETITION

I was suited up for sparring and standing near the ring, breathing wetly through my mouthpiece, the helmet moist around my head.

This was the day I was to spar with Anne. It was her first time in the ring. She was warming up, and she looked at me with wide eyes.

I was nervous, too. I could only grudgingly admit to myself that I felt apprehensive about sparring with a woman. By this time, I had fought women in official bouts, but that was in the strange heated atmosphere of competition, where you don't know your opponent. This was in the close atmosphere of the gym, with a woman I knew.

I secretly worried that sparring a woman would be different—less professional, more fraught with covert emotions, resentments, misunderstandings. With the guys, I know what to expect. They may fear hitting me because I am a woman, but I don't have to worry that they will misinterpret my hitting them. I know they won't take it personally.

With a woman, I feared helplessness used to elicit sympathy; tears used as a weapon; resentments for losing; back-stabbing; misunderstanding the rules, or refusing to follow them. I feared that she would start "acting like a girl," and embarrass and demean both of us. How could I stereotype other women when I hate it so much myself? I felt a sharp mixture of anxiety and shame.

Jess, now accustomed to having me spar, gave me cursory attention. He ran his hand quickly over my back to check if I was wearing my chest protection. (All women boxers are required to wear breast guards, ungainly plastic bras. We wear them under our shirts.) The first time Jess ran his hand over my back this way, I shot him a questioning look. He gestured as if to say, I am a gentleman; I will not touch your chest.

I got in the ring. Anne hopped in after me. A martial-arts student, she recently took up boxing. Through her mouth-piece, she asked me a question. In martial arts, she said, they practice without full contact. In fact, they get penalized if they strike hard. She softly cuffed up the side of my head to show how much they pull their blows. What about sparring in boxing? I responded through my mouth guard: "You don't want to put everything into it, but you want to snap the punch—Like this." I illustrated in the air. Anne watched intently. Then she moved close, intimate. She asked: "Will you hit me, right now?" During this rest time before the bell sounds, this idea seemed foreign, and immensely brave. I didn't do it. Somehow, it seemed wrong.

Anne, I quickly discovered, was a graceful fighter with a long reach, good balance, and solid legs. She had fifteen pounds and three inches on me, and she used her longer arms to advantage. When she popped her jab out, I was left churning on the outside and had to discover ways to get my shorter—albeit more powerful—arms inside. The round ended as educational for me as for her. Later, as she left the ring, we touched our gloved fists together. The gesture was more than perfunctory. I relaxed.

* * * *

Anne and I sparred again. Eventually, I learned her story. She comes from a family of boxers. Her dad was a fighter; so were her brothers. In fact, her great-uncle Fred, an ex-fighter, lawyer, novelist, and journeyman sailor of seventy-plus years, is a fixture at the gym.

Fred must be over six feet tall, weighing in the neighborhood of two hundred pounds, with a balding dome of a head, long ears, immense sloping shoulders, and a large belly. He dresses in old blue sweatpants and a white T-shirt. He sits in the gym chairs after working out, with a towel on his head, passing the time of day with whoever comes along.

Anne said she was always a pacifist. She abhorred violence. But she felt afraid, reliant on the male members of her family for protection. She couldn't compete with them. Getting into martial arts was her first step toward feeling more confident, but something was lacking. When she talked to her family about her feelings of vulnerability, they asked her, "So what's stopping you from learning how to fight?" So Anne, a pacifist, ended up in a boxing gym.

She told me later that stepping into the ring for the first time took an act of courage. When she climbed out, she was deeply relieved. She said she actually felt more nervous the second time. "It was one thing to get hit," she said, laughing. "You beat me up and I proved I can take it. But I'm not so sure I like hitting back."

I understood what she meant. Maybe that's what aggression means to many of us, who were taught to be defenseless.

The second time we sparred, we had a great time. After one interesting exchange—with Anne using her reach to perfect advantage—the bell rang, and she said breathlessly, "That was a really good session." I felt warm, slightly embarrassed by my past worries.

Anne left for college within a few months. She has a picture of us, taken right after sparring, with arms slung round each other.

I'm beginning to think my fears about fighting other women are more about my sexism than about reality. There is still a part of me that believes a woman boxer won't be as good as a man. I have to beat her, decisively, or I lose face. If she beats me, I have no hope of competing on a man's level.

I know it is wrong to feel this way. Yet I wonder how much of it actually signals a leap of faith. Finally, I am comparing my abilities not as much to other women as to men.

With that, I discover an entire new world of insecurity.

Women are narcissistic and backbiting. Women fight over beauty and social status. Women gossip maliciously and use emotion as a weapon. Women can't shake hands and walk away. Women don't know how to fight fair.

I've always bought into these ideas. Certainly I could think of women who fit at least some of these descriptions.

But if I thought about it, I could also name plenty of men who have the same traits—men who are vain, whether preening over job status or looks; men who manipulate others with guilt; men who talk behind other people's backs; men who don't fight fair; men who are just plain lousy at competing.

It wasn't until after sparring with women that I really began to question my beliefs about female competition. The idea that we resort to tears and temper tantrums when confronted with the slightest conflict seems based on the assumption that we are less equipped to handle aggression. Confronted with competition—which requires a controlled aggression—it's assumed that we will fall apart.

One thing that sometimes gets lost in discussions of gender differences with respect to aggression is the plasticity of human behavior. People are quick studies, and they can adapt to a surprising number of situations. A ten-year-old girl discouraged from forthright competition by her parents may feel uncomfortable on the first day of soccer practice, but by the tenth, she will probably be charging about with glee. A woman executive at first unaccustomed to hard-edged business dealings can soon find herself mentally rubbing her hands together delightedly as she takes on the opposition.

In my conversations with women involved in aggressive arenas, this adaptability is always part of their story. In a matter of weeks, Anne went from being a person who was afraid of physical conflict to one who felt confident with it—and was good at it.

As with so many other areas of aggression, assumptions about female competition shatter under close examination.

Even when male and female behavior is similar in this realm, it seems we interpret it far differently. Women are often not recognized for their ability to handle conflicts. In one study, managers were asked about their secretaries' relationships. They described them as backbiting and catty. When asked themselves, the secretaries said they got along just fine.[1]

What is considered healthy competition in men can be seen as backbiting in women. A spat between two men won't be thought of as a catfight, even if voices are raised or stormy and sulky brows appear. The same spat between two women can set a group buzzing with the news, complete with laughing acquaintances swiping the air with their fingers, making meowing noises.

Men are just as governed by expectations of forthright competition as women are by expectations of incompetence. Self-help books on raising boys, such as *Raising a Son: Parents and the Makings of a Healthy Man* by Don and Jeanne Elium, cast every boy as a rugged little troublemaker (a "testosterone beast") who needs a firm hand in controlling his natural aggression. But how many boys would rather play in the school band or be on the debating team than on the football team? How many are shy and easily wounded? How many shrink from conflict?

Just as a boy who doesn't fit the standard of a testosterone beast can be called a sissy, the woman who goes against the stereotypes can be derisively characterized, as well. Young, she is a tomboy. Older, depending on how far she takes it, she is labeled a Jane Wayne, a butch. She threatens men, but she also threatens women.

While men are frequently blamed for enforcing these stereotypes, I believe women are responsible as well. In his book *Women's Sports: A History*, author Allen Guttmann cites an experiment where male and female college students were shown slides of female bodybuilders. The men consistently judged the women bodybuilders as much more attractive than the women did. In a similar study, two women were described in identical terms, except one was said to be a bodybuilder. Women rated the bodybuilder less feminine than the men did. The women also suspected her of homosexuality.

It may have been that the women in these studies were trying to anticipate what men consider attractive, and getting it wrong. Or maybe their judgments demonstrate that women are socialized to find masculine attributes in other women even more unappealing than men are taught to.

In the past, stereotypes about female competition may have served the purpose of maintaining strictures against open female aggression. But these stereotypes also kept women out of highly competitive fields such as law and politics, and they continue to undermine our professional credibility.

Today, enough women are entering competitive fields to challenge the stereotypes, making it obvious they are no longer accurate, if they ever were. Younger girls especially are witnessing a revolution. Women are coming together to compete, in public and on a major level, for the first time in recent memory—in sports.

They are seeing it with their own eyes: The girls on the team aren't any different from the boys.

Twelve ⟶

WOMEN IN SPORTS

It was between the second and third round of my first fight, in Yakima, Washington. My chest felt like a husk, hollow and empty, with my breath gone. The round had just ended, the referee stepping quickly between us, and I turned toward my corner. The world was hot, electric—little sparks seemed to snap in the air. I lowered myself onto the stool, and Jess jumped in the ring, white towel in hand. He began wiping my face, and the towel turned bright red—blood, running from my nose. "Raise your head," he ordered me roughly, and I tilted my face to a sudden flash of light: Water sluiced down, washing blood into my mouth, over my shirt, in pale trickles down my arms, a spray of tiny drops across the canvas.

Jess didn't bother saying much, this round. It was obvious I was hopelessly outclassed. I was losing badly.

There was a moment during the second round when I found myself wishing the fight was over. I was surprised to realize that I had almost given up hope.

Jess gave me a final brusque wipe with the towel, then reinserted my mouthpiece. The bell rang again: final round.

The referee, a faceless figure in blinding white, beckoned us close to touch gloves. My opponent looked down at me with puzzled hazel eyes. She used me as a punching bag the entire fight, but I took her hardest blows without falling. Now she was tired and confused.

As we began fighting again, I realized how winded she was, but it felt too late to take advantage. In retrospect, this feeling made no sense: My wind was still there, my legs solid and fresh, while hers were starting to wobble. But I had already taken a beating, and she was still capable of delivering one. Hard, crunching blows fell as the referee hung over my shoulder—always close but, in terms of the fight, endlessly far away—to ascertain if I was okay. Yes. Each blow was like the sun a moment before eclipse, a second before the world goes out.

I finally backed her up against the ropes. The crowd was screaming, a huge noise that splintered into small, specific pieces of advice: "Go to the body." "Don't let her back you up, girl." When she was trapped in the corner, I began unleashing body shots. Her stomach was soft, and the flesh yielded as I punched under her ribs—I felt as if I could touch the inside of her spine. Her face drained to a sudden milky color, and she squirmed out of the corner to dance away, eyes shocked.

It seemed that we had spent our entire lives in this fight and that it would never end. I had become stuck on the go button. Blows rained down on me as I pressed forward, until finally she was once again against the ropes, defiant, daring me once again to cross the expanse of her long, deadly arms. A smear of my blood adorned each of her gloves.

The final bell rang.

Jess was quiet when I went back to my corner. All around me a huge silence roared. My gloves and helmet were taken off, my hands unwrapped. It was time for the decision, and the referee held us, hand by hand, in the middle of the ring. They announced the winner—red corner, her corner—and she picked up the trophy with a look of wild joy. I was suddenly happy for her, and happy for me—the fight was over. We hugged tightly, steaming shirts pressed together, and she said "Good fight" in my ear. I nodded, knowing that my pain at losing would come soon enough, but that it really had nothing to do with her.

As we left the arena floor—a high school gymnasium— Chuck said, "Well, back to the drawing board." Alone in the makeshift girls' locker room (the janitor's shower), I crumpled to my knees, bawling like a baby. The shame at losing was sharp and deep. I felt nothing toward my opponent—no anger, no envy. I felt only this pain so encompassing, it was more like grief.

When I left the locker room, the team was waiting. We went to a restaurant, to return later for more fights. I kept my head bowed. The guys retracted from me, awkward in my loss. In the restaurant, Jess was also ill at ease. All he said was, "I guess we learned you can take a punch." But Isaac, one of the fighters, came up behind me to place a warm hand on my shoulder momentarily.

That night, while flies buzzed outside the gymnasium doors, I sat on the bleachers, watching the young girls horse around after their fights. There were several twelve- and thirteen-year-olds, laughing and comfortable. From watching them play, it was impossible to tell which of them won and which lost. I thought about the level of confidence—of personal responsibility—it takes to lose a contest and still respect yourself, as well as the victor.

I thought about these young girls, and I questioned if their comfort was particular to their personal circumstances or if it signaled a transition in the making, a new ease with female aggression in sports.

I thought about how it was, after all, just a game.

* * * *

Women have long engaged in sports, from aristocratic women riding in the hunt to such lower-class nineteenth-century women as the "famous boxing woman of Billingsgate," as writer Allen Guttmann discusses in his book *Women's Sports*.

The middle-class woman, however, has historically been prohibited financially and socially from pursuing the elite sports of the rich, at the same time as she has been discouraged from the rough sports of the lower classes. Sports for the majority of women were nearly nonexistent until recently.

The most seemingly inconsequential development can be the impetus for major change. Nearly a century ago, the bicycle liberated women in more ways than one. There was a newly realized sense of freedom—to ride unchaperoned and free—that inspired some women to challenge social constraints, including the damper of heavy clothing worn at the time.

How women feel about their bodies, and how society feels about women using them in competition, is not just a matter of fashion. That women are entering sports long defined as male—rough, full-bore, competitive contact sports—has consequences far removed from athletics.

My first fight came not long after I started training. I had little ring experience. I honestly didn't have much of an idea of what I was doing. I think Jess assumed that other women couldn't fight and that I would therefore have an easy win. He told me much later that he knew we were in trouble the moment he saw her throw her right hand. I'm embarrassed now to think about it, but in that fight I took a beating without returning much myself. All I could say afterward was, *I didn't go down.*

I spent the next few weeks out of the gym, nursing my sore pride—and a very sore head. A headache plagued me for weeks like a wet spider in the front of my skull. I could barely think, and any exercise set up a painful throbbing. After two weeks of this, I was convinced I needed to see a doctor.

I went to a neurologist. It was a mistake, because I didn't learn much besides the fact that I am a stubborn person—and no one needed to tell me that.

The neurologist boinked my knees with tongs, made me twiddle my fingers and touch my nose, and then pronounced that I didn't show any damage, but that the pain clearly meant something. He told me not to compete for at least several weeks, if ever again. He gave me a stern lecture about head injuries. Migraine headaches run in my family, I had told him, and he pointed out that I could easily trigger a lifelong problem. The best idea, he said, was not to compete again. Morose, I took his diagnosis to Jess, then sent a copy off for the insurance that all amateur boxers get with their registration. I was worried about the injury, and I probably overstated its importance on the form myself.

The insurance company paid the cost of the bill, but I paid with my boxing credentials. The decision came down that I could no longer compete. Apparently, someone in the local amateur boxing association had called the neurologist and he had said competition wouldn't be the brightest idea in the world.

To make a long story short, all it took was the disappearance of the headache to make me miss the gym, and miss the idea of trying again. A bit of carping on my part, a visit to a different doctor—who gave me a clean bill of health—and I was eventually allowed back in the ring.

I still question whether the neurologist was reacting more to my gender than to my headache. I found out later that "boxer's headache" is well known. If I had been a man, would he have suggested that I stop fighting? I don't know. Neurologists generally aren't big boxing fans.

But he was a doctor, and I am not trying to undermine his medical authority. Even a mild headache may signal injury, even permanent damage. It placed a little ticking bomb next to my pillow, saying, You can't do this forever. Don't do this forever. I told myself: A year. The year passed, and I was still in the gym, preparing for yet another fight. I felt I wanted to redeem myself, although I'm not sure why.

The headache put a pall over my boxing that would never quite lift: the curse of possible injury. In moments of worry after a fight or sparring, I would sit quietly, silently feeling for a tightness around my skull, asking myself if I was getting dull, wondering if I was evincing the first signs of lasting damage.

Those who dislike women boxing, or hate the sport to begin with, will wince at the thought of women getting hurt. I am not going to deny that injury in boxing—as in many sports—is a real and viable issue. That is why I am writing about my experience with headaches, though part of me wants to pretend it didn't happen.

It did happen. Boxing is a dangerous sport, as much for women as for men. There was an older fighter who hung around the gym for a time. Half of his face had gone slack, with one eye staring off into space. Sometimes he spoke in a thick slur. It was obvious some neurological damage had occurred. Whether this was a result of boxing or of his rough life (he had supposedly been in many a street fight) was unclear. His reflexes were gone, and on the rare occasions when someone would let him in the ring—which they shouldn't have—he would get hit constantly.

Watching a fighter like that your skin crawls, because there is something so unnatural about the person's lack of reflex: It makes the limbs seem flat and dead.

The growing acceptance of women in sports means women get hurt, just like men—from minor injuries to fatalities. A woman race-car driver is killed. A woman jockey is thrown and paralyzed for life. Someday on the horizon, a woman boxer will be left in a coma or stuttering thickly through a slack mouth. It makes many uncomfortable, but I think it's an important right to grant—that women should also have the opportunity to throw their personal safety to the winds to pursue a sport.

A leading reason women are taking on serious roles in sports is school athletics. In this realm, few laws can compare in social impact to Title IX of the federal Education Act of 1972. Title IX prohibits sex discrimination in all federally funded educational programs and activities.

Schools had long rejected and refused to budget sports for girls. Under this act, they were required to remedy a system that had been terribly unequal.

I was just entering school myself when Title IX was passed, and I grew up in the midst of the turmoil it created. At my grade school, efforts to involve girls in athletics were erratic. One girls' gym class was led by a tall, skinny teacher who did what she had been doing for the past thirty years: Put students through bust-exercise drills. For competition, there was Ping-Pong. Another teacher, however, threw open the gymnasium doors to let us play touch football with the boys.

Though the act was passed in 1972, the Department of Health, Education and Welfare allowed a three-year phase-in. At the end of this phase-in, controversy over Title IX was still so intense that public hearings had to be held. Football coaches reared on their hind legs to assert that the law would destroy intercollegiate sports by taking money away from lucrative male teams and throwing it needlessly at unprofitable women's teams. A spokeswoman for an intercollegiate women's athletic league hit the nail on the head when she summarized their arguments as "no more than a plea that discrimination against women be permitted to continue because it is profitable to men or institutions. . . ."[1]

The fear that equal opportunity would hurt male sports has since proven false. The law has increased athletic programs for women without diminishing sports for men.

While Title IX has made huge gains possible, its implementation has been hampered by lack of enforcement. Some schools try to find ways to squirm around its requirements. At one rural high school, for instance, girls lobbying for their own soccer team were told that their school had already met legal requirements for female athletes. It turned out that the school was counting *cheerleading*, of all things, as a sport. Without cheerleading, girls actually made up less than a third of the school's athletes.[2]

The numbers of girls getting involved in school athletics still lags. In 1994, over 3.4 million boys competed in high school sports, compared with just over 2.1 million girls—a substantial number of girls, but still substantially lower than the number of boys.[3]

The Centers for Disease Control and Prevention recently found that girls exercise less as they get older, going from active grade-schoolers to sedentary high school seniors. This trend is most pronounced among girls from low-income schools.[4]

However unrealistic, boys are encouraged to use sports as a means to escape from poverty, but usually girls are not. Community centers and charities focus on helping boys in sports, from boxing to basketball, while girls are ignored. Without safe parks or luxuries such as swimming pools, girls from poor neighborhoods find few opportunities to exercise.

Title IX may demand girls have the same athletic opportunities, but it can't force communities and families to support such activities. It's unusual to see a girls' team with the crowds, glorification, and attention—not to mention cheerleaders—that the boys' teams get. This lack of encouragement must be detrimental to their spirits. In addition, girls' teams are frequently relegated to club status, which is not funded by schools, while boys' teams are promoted to varsity status, and amply funded even when they run in the red.

To remedy inequities in sports, parents have to get involved. This does seem to be happening more. But schools need to offer girls more options, especially with regard to contact sports.

When schools do offer girls contact sports, it seems that girls take up the challenge with a vengeance. An example of this is rugby, one of the fastest-growing college sports for women. Parents stand on the sidelines, cheering as their daughters run full-bore into one another, smashing heads together in group scrums. Fathers and mothers yell advice along with admonishments: "Don't cut your face—graduation's in two weeks." The young women, for their part, seem to revel in the experience of muddy competition, and the reputation of rugby players as hard-drinking, rowdy athletes.[5]

As long as girls are not only less likely to be involved in athletics but are also actively discouraged from pursuing most direct contact "male" sports, like rugby or soccer, social beliefs in gendered aggression will remain. I can't help but think that those girls are at a disadvantage, because they've been denied the experience of one-on-one direct competition and teamwork (especially as skills to be rewarded) and may lack confidence in their abilities.

Crucial to good sportsmanship is not only learning how to compete but also how to lose. In boxing, the spectator may feel embarrassed for the losing fighter, but those inside the fight game are remarkably at ease about loss. They find little shame in it—disappointment, but not shame. Losing can be a brutal character builder, but boys have gained from it while girls have not.

In Madeleine Blais's account of a high school girls' basketball team, *In These Girls, Hope Is a Muscle*, a mother muses over her athletic daughter: "Just think what it must be like to go through puberty and have your body on your side." I believe the validation of women athletes means a great deal for our culture—not just in terms of physical pride but also with regard to the breakdown of gender segregation throughout society. Such approbation gives women a sense of entitlement that is not left in the gymnasium but is carried outside its doors.

The night air in Yakima, Washington, was velvety and dry, like flour dust. Driving through town after the fights, the smell of hay blew through the van window. I was riding with Isaiah's family to the hotel.

I had been riding with them the entire trip. As we left the gym that morning—after I was cussed out by Chuck for having a bowl of Cheerios and drinking two glasses of water before the official weigh-in—Jess informed me I was to ride with Isaiah's family.

Isaiah is perhaps twelve, a sturdy young boxer with a somber poise. His mother is a large woman with delicate features. His father is as sturdy as his son, and he talks incessantly. They have a little girl, perhaps five or six, who, like her brother, acts much older than her years.

Everyone else on my team was in another van, along with a team from the Warm Springs Indian reservation that had met up with us that morning at the gym. Though Isaiah's family was kind and their minivan comfortable, I felt excluded from my team. Pulling away from the curb that morning, the other fighters and Jess looked crammed yet comfortable piled into the Warm Springs team's battered white van. As the sun rose above Portland, we followed them out of town, up the Columbia River gorge. Isaiah's mother handed out cold chicken to her youngest (Isaiah, fighting, was forbidden food or drink until after the weigh-in) as the windows of the van misted up with the cold dew of morning.

We followed the Columbia, a huge river that cuts a dramatic slice out of the Cascade mountain range. Waterfalls jettison over massive cliffs and the mountains are covered with Douglas fir. You can drive for hours up the gorge, your car a little speck along the freeway, buffeted by wind. As you drive east, the terrain grows slowly drier, the trees sparser, the hills sandier, until mile after mile of the distant mountains seem bereft of growth, the dunny color of sage in the distance.

We finally crossed the river to head straight north into Yakima, which is tucked in the parched hills of eastern Washington. Even in March, the land was waterless, compared with the loamy dampness of Portland. We drove past sad farms—the kind with a few dozen acres and an old double-wide trailer. Isaiah's sister cooed at the dusty goats.

Hours later—after the fights that evening—we pulled into the motel. It was one of those big, cheap, sprawling affairs, the kind with rooms built courtyard-style around the parking lot.

The boys spilled out of the other van. Together with the Warm Springs team and the coaches, there were perhaps twenty of us. The boys ranged in age from nine to eighteen, and they had treated the trip as an exciting outing. The Warm Springs fighters were quiet boys with brush-cut hair, wearing the cheap cotton tank tops available in every discount store that summer; the deeply cut armpits exposed swaths of bright skin. The youngest couldn't have been more than nine years old and all of sixty-five pounds. Their coach, a bony man in cowboy boots, seemed edgy and talkative.

Jess had rented several rooms, and after he opened them with his keys, the boys ran pell-mell, choosing which rooms they would sleep in. Doors were flung open, pouring orange light into the darkness. Isaiah's family disappeared by themselves into one room. The coaches made sure each room was supervised by either a coach or another adult so that there would be no goofing around.

It became clear that I was a major concern. Where would I sleep? The problem seemed to puzzle the men.

I waited patiently by the van, listening to the distant sound of the highway. Finally, Jess signaled me toward one of the rooms. I went in and found two beds, empty and flat. In a few seconds, Jess followed. He was leading Octavio, my sparring partner, and Octavio's friend Isaac, a heavyset young man with a broad, friendly face. They looked at me with trepidation, smiled at the floor. Neither spoke English.

Jess said we would all be sharing the room. Everyone's eyes fell on the two beds. The beds were narrow, covered with cheap rust-colored blankets pulled tightly across the pillows, and separated only by a tiny night table. We filled up the small space immediately, with barely enough room to maneuver around without knocking elbows. We were all aware of the closeness of the room. There wasn't much space on the floor, either. Two beds, and there were four of us.

Battered from my first fight, tired from the night spent waiting on a hard bench, and emotionally exhausted, I decided to let Jess figure this one out. I went to the bathroom, washed my face, took out my contacts, brushed my teeth, and ended up burying a used sanitary napkin wrapped in toilet paper deep in my gym bag, because there was no trash can.

In the mirror, my face looked gray, with stress-paled skin and bloodshot eyes surrounded with dark circles. My eyelids and chin were bruised, the bridge of my nose swollen and tight, my lips puffy, the inside of my mouth lacerated and sore. When I was done using the bathroom, I wiped up all vestiges of my presence. In this befuddled state, with the soft voices of the men carrying through the door, it seemed of great importance that I not leave evidence of my period or person behind. Even with the bathroom door between us, the close quarters pressed.

When I stepped back into the room, I found the men all sitting on one bed, watching television. The tension in the room suddenly became acute. Octavio and Isaac had probably never been in the same bedroom with an unrelated older woman.

I suddenly saw why Jess was chaperoning us. Not because they might actually have tried something, but because without his presence, the room might have become unbearable with secret tensions and magnetic fears.

Gesturing grandly at Octavio, Jess informed me that the young man wouldn't let me sleep on the floor: I must take one of the beds. Jess took the other bed, and the two young men prepared to sleep on the floor. I thanked them and crawled in between the sheets, still dressed in jeans and a T-shirt. They sat there on the bed opposite mine—no more than inches away—paralyzed. No one moved for a few seconds. Finally, Jess sighed, then turned off the light. There was a soft chorus of good nights, in Spanish and English.

I could hear one of the young men rustling, getting ready to sleep on the floor beside me. I felt I could reach out and touch him. It was with this thought in mind that I turned into the sheets and fell suddenly asleep.

In the morning, I woke slowly and listened to the sounds of the other fighters talking to one another outside the hotel window. With my eyes still closed, I heard Jess calling me gently.

When I sat up, I found the men still on the floor. They were waking up. Octavio was curled half into my sleeping bag. One of his arms was entangled in the black cord. Jess told me, "Octavio hopes you don't mind that he used your sleeping bag. He didn't have one."

147

"No, I don't mind," I said. I looked down at Octavio, half-listening as some of the other young fighters burst in on us, all full of the morning. They were talking as they brushed their teeth, and bragging, bragging, bragging.

Carlos, one of the older fighters, emerged abruptly from our bathroom. He was holding my tube of toothpaste aloft, like a trophy.

There is an unease over women in sports that goes deeper than the issue of mere physical competition. It's an unease that also manifests itself in the exclusion of women from other all-male enclaves, where men will go to extreme trouble to keep their world free of women.

Some analysts label this "misogyny." But I don't believe that most men in these situations hate women. They would tell you that they love their wives and daughters. There are men who will grant respect to each individual woman who enters their world but who still adamantly stand against all others—what I think of as the "you're not like the others" phenomenon.

They don't hate women. They feel uncomfortable with us, or at least they believe they should. Jokes about male bonding aside, I don't believe most men in all-male groups feel a special kinship with the others that is reliant on the group staying male-only. Had I not been in that hotel room that night, Jess and the boys probably wouldn't have partaken in any mysterious rituals. They would have done exactly the same thing—sleep—only they would have felt a lot easier doing it.

Women fighting to enter all-male realms have met ugly attacks, and there is something in the image of female linebackers that scares people, because it is so unfeminine.

For the most part, though, the quick acceptance of women once they finally make it into once-all-male institutions suggests that it is fear of the unknown that motivates exclusion. Older men in particular fuss over "female problems," such as menstruation, while younger men worry over being judged and found wanting. The positive experience of the integration of women into institutions such as federal military academies shows that these fears are, as the *New York Times* said, "as baseless as they are sexist."[6]

Many still seem to expect that women's motivation to aggress is political, rather than personal (most young men playing football aren't doing so as a political statement). The lack of lofty aspirations among such women can be frustrating to some journalists who are looking for each woman weight lifter or marine to have a reason for what she is doing that is far better thought-out than that of any man in her position.

But a lot of these women don't want to be singled out. For them, being part of their team or troop is what is important, and a focus on their sex only undermines that.

I think these women are saying something important. In the past, women athletes thought in political terms. They had to. They were the first. They were breaking the barriers. Now enough women have entered some of these fields that this inordinate focus on gender is diminishing. Women are joining the team for all the ordinary reasons that men do, and they are asking to be allowed to play first as athletes, second as women.

Bit by bit, girls will become as athletic as boys. Women's basketball careers won't end automatically after college. Women's professional sports teams will gain more and more credibility, until someday we will have female sports megacelebrities on a par with Michael Jordan.

Then the posters adorning teenagers' bedroom walls will include women: basketball players with tree-trunk legs and splooshy shoes, posed against the detergent colors of marketing, or maybe even posters of women boxers with the animal grace of Sugar Ray Leonard. Then girls as well as boys will tentatively rehearse to themselves the roar of the crowd, the elation of victory, the pain of loss.

These girls won't be like boys. They will not become more aggressive—not each and every one of them, any more than the boys they know. What they will become is more involved in the world around them, and more recognized for having a variety of traits and skills.

Someday the last holdouts—the locker rooms and hotel rooms, the barracks and bivouacs—will include women. We will materialize not just in the midst of aggression but in the midst of personal relationships with men, as equals.

Maybe then some of the paternalism that so often marks relationships between men and women will subside, leaving in its place not just equal responsibility but the firm foundation for warmer relationships—a common ground where men and women can meet as adults, friends, and lovers.

Thirteen ✦

AGGRESSION AND EROS

The Grand Avenue is the only gym in town that trains both amateur and professional boxers. The two work side by side but live different lives.

The professionals' training is more intensive because they must be able to go at least ten rounds, compared to amateurs, whose bouts are limited to only three. The physical conditioning it takes to go the distance in a professional fight is amazing. A twelve-round bout can last forty-seven minutes, counting the one-minute rest between each round. The thirty-six minutes spent boxing can be compared with dancing very fast while carrying dumbbells in each hand (many people don't realize how heavy even ten-ounce gloves can be, especially after a few rounds). Then there is the exhaustion following adrenaline bursts, and the punishment of being hit.

The majority of people, even those who run daily, couldn't last two minutes in the ring, let alone ten to twelve rounds of such—there isn't a better word for it—*violent* exercise.

Because they are in such peak condition, good professional boxers make it look easier than it is. Fans are amazed when so many professionals quickly put on weight after winning a title. It's easy to forget that the fighter has trained constantly—hours a day, day after day—for years while fighting his way up, all the while starving himself to make weight. He's probably sick and tired of it and wants a break.

Such training is astounding to watch. There are a couple of professionals who come into the Grand when training for a fight. Featherweight Miguel Arrozal is one. For a few months, another ranked professional preparing for a title fight was training at the gym.

Another, Mario, was in line to fight for a junior featherweight title. He is a small, spare man with a quiet presence, wiry, like all featherweights. His natural street weight is probably closer to 135 pounds than 122, the uppermost limit for the match he was training for. He has clear skin the color of resin, a square face with a mashed-in boxer's nose, and a sleek head with black seal-like hair cut close. He lives in Mexico, but his manager sent him to train here.

I got to spar with Mario when he had a few rounds to spare, and he didn't mind playing around with a novice. Getting ready for his match, he worked round after round in the ring. I was disquieted as the time got closer to his fight and his trainer didn't seem interested in bringing in professional sparring partners.

It would have been an expense to fly a sparring partner in from another city, but there wasn't anyone in the gym of his caliber for him to work with. Mario's title fight was against a tricky southpaw, and the only southpaw at the Grand is Damion, an amateur. Damion is easily the classiest fighter in the gym, in my view—he's fought over seventy times. Once he threw a right to my belly that knocked the wind out of me; it was like getting kicked in the stomach by a horse. I saw him floor an opponent with a similar blow at a tournament, and I found myself nearly out of my chair with excitement.

Mario should be working with professionals. Working with amateurs, he ended up teaching more than learning, since no one could really press him, test his reflexes, make him work on a strategy. A professional needs to hit with power, and working with amateurs, Mario couldn't do that.

When I got in the ring with Mario, he worked on his defense. One day he joked when I climbed in, and all I could catch of his remarks in Spanish was *chicaquita*—"girl." Jess translated for me, laughing. "He says please don't hit him so hard this time," and everyone joined in the joke.

I bring up Mario because when he first came to this country, he developed a minor crush on me—or so his people said, since he doesn't speak English. Jess teased us, saying that Mario only worked with me in the ring because he wanted to smell my perfume, and I rolled my eyes at this, because during a workout, all I smell of is sweat. And with a face as red as a hot poker, sometimes with glove marks, I'm not exactly a picture of beauty.

The interest, if it existed, didn't last. Maybe when a woman in a boxing gym was a new idea, and presented many interesting implications, Mario might have made suggestive remarks. I doubt my sweaty face held appeal for long. Besides, I hear he's married and has several children in Mexico. And he never acted anything but a gentleman.

I got in the ring with Mario, and I could feel it in my feet the fact that he—at least once—thought of me in a sexual sense. It gave a new sense to the grip of canvas, to the feeling of his damp shirt under my arm, to the snuffling sound of my nose against his neck as I moved in close and practiced on my inside work.

The rounds passed as Mario danced gracefully, avoiding my clumsy attack. I must not have been acting peculiar, because between rounds Jess only chastised me for not working the body enough and said that otherwise I was doing well.

It's easy to do well when your sparring partner won't hit you back—really hit you back. Mario, as befitted his status, only acted namby-pamby, babying me lightly with his fist. I gestured rudely at my face with my glove, the boxer's non-verbal way of saying, Hit me, goddamn it. Now why did I go and do that? He sent his left out soft and poky-looking, but it had a serious sting at the end of it, and my eyes promptly started watering. His eyes seemed only soft, though, and completely unafraid.

As he worked, Mario made a soft, *shhhh*ing sound, which sharpened into a hiss every time he threw a blow. I have wondered if part of the reason boxers make a sound every time they throw a punch is not only to quicken or add power to their blows—and to ensure that they are breathing properly, since it's easy to hold your breath in the ring without thinking—but also as a psychological weapon. Mario's humming, whispery sound took on an eerie, impersonal tone, like a snake ready to strike. There is something daunting in knowing that the blows can be as limitless as this breath, hissing and sharp.

When I burrowed in and repeatedly hooked my left fist into his belly, he only twisted lightly and gently thudded my belly with his own fist, letting me know: You are open there.

"Stop shoving," Jess ordered from the side of the ring, annoyed that I was pushing against Mario while inside, instead of tucking my head into his neck proper and keeping my balance.

I left the ring after a few rounds. Mario got out, too, wet and worn-out and hard around the mouth. He paced, breathing hard, as his trainer unlaced his gloves and belt.

Mario, standing, tilted his hips forward so the trainer could pull the belt down. I was a few feet away, with Jess unlatching the strap of my helmet. My hair rose with static as he pulled the headgear off. Mario looked over, laughed, said something. Jess laughed, as well, then turned to me to translate. "He says," Jess said, "you are the queen."

Sports, boxing, hard physical labor—all can be intensely erotic. Anytime people use their bodies, they can become sensual and aware of them. Women runners and other athletes talk about how the joy of physical expression knows few boundaries—the pleasure of using one's body in sports easily carries over to sexuality.

Exercise enhances people's sex lives not just because it makes them more confident about their bodies but also because it heightens physical awareness. The nerve endings seem sharper, the mouth more perceptive to taste.

In contact sports, this sensuality can be even stronger. I don't mean necessarily sexual, but physically intense, the form of eroticism that can occur without sexual arousal.

Even in the hardest sparring bouts, the pain of being punched can exist in another realm. The thud of a fighter's fist against the mouth can make a sound like creaking, but without the fear attached to being struck, it only clarifies this sensuality. The intimacy of contact is distilled. For all the learned responses in boxing, it never seems artificial, and so the direct contact of it—the rubbing of bodies, the clinching, and, of course, the punching—can feel perfectly natural, deeply sensual, all within the astringent atmosphere of a boxing gym.

It is easy, in a culture where adult women and men rarely touch unless they are having sex, to confuse this with sexuality. The lack of touching among adults can charge even a slight physical contact, a mistletoe kiss, with sexual meaning.

Any bodily contact can become erotic: Some mothers experience deeply sensual sensations, even orgasms, while nursing their children. I think some marital fighting occurs out of a need for conflict and the intimacy of resolution—the need for something, anything, to happen.

I am self-conscious as I write this, knowing that discussing the relationships among eroticism, sexuality, and violence is going to make me vulnerable to all sorts of criticism, such as that I am into kinky sex or view sex as a sport. (We forget, though, that sports can give the same spiritual elation as prayer.)

The overlapping areas between sex and aggression are equated with negative violence—rape, child molestation, incest—or crude copulation, not lovemaking.

But I think there is a whole other realm to the eroticism of aggression. Our definitions of aggression, the actions directed toward another, are close to our definitions of sexuality: the flush and demands of desire. Many of the expressions used to define aggressiveness—"determined," "an energetic pursuit of one's ends," "full of initiative, or enterprising," "marked by forceful energy"—can also be used to describe sexual need.

A sexuality without an aggressive urge, in my mind, would be a sexuality devoid of action and energy—a sexuality without passion, without desire.

The selfishness associated with aggressive desire can be positive. It can tell our partners we desire them intensely; it reaffirms pleasure in our bodies; it fills us with a sense of confidence.

We often hear that women need to be more sexually aggressive. There have been countless books examining how women's sexuality has been made passive and inert.

Yet within certain spheres, we have long recognized the sexually assertive woman. In my grandmother's time, a woman was supposed to remain pure of desire until her wedding night, when all was supposed to dissolve, as author Rita Mae Brown puts it, into a happy yes. Housewives in the 1950s were advised to wrap their naked bodies in cellophane and greet their husbands at the door, among other demeaning methods to spice up their love lives.

Today, women are allowed—and encouraged—to be sexually aggressive in a wider range of relationships, including sex outside of marriage. Articles in women's magazines advise us to demand what we want in bed, ask men out on dates, to "be the sexual aggressor."

I do think that this recognition of female desire is a step forward. But I also question if it signals another way in which our aggression isn't taken seriously. No one tells men to get more sexually demanding. We assume they already are. We also worry that once kindled, their aggression might take on a negative expression. For women, aggression in bed is not linked with predatory violence, but with playfulness—and especially, male pleasure.

Despite all the talk about sexual assertiveness, our sexual needs are still supposed to occur within safe perimeters—marriage, a relationship with a trusted lover—and in this manner, views of female sexuality have not changed much at all. In the past decade or so, we seem to have retreated even more from allowing women sexual confidence, confusing a sense of entitlement to pleasure with vulnerability to AIDS, violence, and other possible dangers.

But it is hard to contain desires into neat compartments. The glow of warm pleasure from exercise is akin to the suffused relaxation following sex. Contact between bodies can imprint on the mind, and what is devoid of sexuality one moment—the impact and joy of a soccer game—can later come rising out of the memory, make the body restless, so that hours later, as one friend put it, you are *randy*.

I usually do not feel a shred of sexuality at the gym. The guys are just other fighters. But there have been times when someone might make an intimate remark, or the light catches someone's back just so, and I am suddenly aware of the rich animal sensuality of the place.

It is the images, odors, and sensations we encounter daily that shape sexuality more than the sex act itself, which is, after all, a pretty limited part of our lives. In this way, the experiences of the gym become a rich sensual history. Each image, each smell—hair oil beaded with sweat, a broken glove, the bitter aftertaste of cologne rubbed off in the ring—is effortlessly stored away, and what occurred without a thought of sex at the time, I can later look back at and find a history of sensation.

There are times when I have gone home from boxing with a voluptuousness of muscle that becomes a strong desire: I feel like a glowing battery containing a hidden germ of danger. The soaked, cold gym clothes translate into tactile nubbed cotton, soaking through to the car seat, dampening the collar of my jacket. Getting ready for the shower, I pull my panties, soaked through with rank-smelling sweat, off pale muscle and goose-bumped flesh. Even peeling off the stained boxing shoes is charged with small pangs of tired sensation, almost excruciating—the cloth being pushed down over ankles, my fingers aching as I gently tug each lace from its eye. Then the time comes when I am standing there, naked and trembling, almost too tired to move but full of aimless desire, as lazy and sharpened as a dead-eye cat.

Sex and boxing, like sex and all sports, have had an uneasy relationship. Sex can get tied up with genuine detriments to young athletes: late nights, booze, drugs. It's easier for the trainers to veto it all rather than single one out for exception.

It is amusing, in this environment which is supposed to be so masculine, that the men involved can live such Spartan lives. The fighter who is being serious about his training can rival any monk for his moral and physical purity. He doesn't drink, smoke, do drugs, stay up past ten o'clock, or have sex, even with his wife, when training for a fight. The fighter who is not being serious—messing with cocaine, alcohol, girls—is common enough to be unremarkable, but he is still held up as an example of someone who wasn't man enough when temptation called.

Getting ready for a fight in a few weeks, Jess finally raised the nerve to talk to me about something that I could tell had been troubling him for some time. "You know," he began, then went on to tell me that when male fighters have sex, they end up losing power in their legs. "Their legs get all soft," he said. Sex is bad for a competing fighter.

It's an old wives' tale, and I don't buy it. But I found myself torn between cynicism and a desire to obey my coach. This obedience was newly discovered—I have never felt such a strong inclination to obey orders before, especially not in conjunction with feelings of self-reliance. For me, obedience has always been tied to loss of dignity, but I discover, as undoubtedly soldiers or other athletes do, that it can coexist with a strong sense of self. The best soldiers or athletes are those who can take orders without feeling debased by it.

Jess went on to tell me he doesn't know how "it" is for women—the effects of sex—but said it is best to play it safe. Meaning, no sex before fights.

"From now on," he told me, "when I say you have a fight coming up, I don't want to have to say anything else, okay?"

I asked him, "For how long?"

Jess took this question calmly. Now he had a woman actually admitting to him, in so many words, that she has sex. He seemed to react to this news, like the entire conversation, with consternation, and a warm, intimate pleasure.

"Two weeks," he said.

"Okay," I said.

He reached out, suddenly, and punched me in the shoulder. It was a hard, affectionate blow. The imprints left by his knuckles stung.

"And I don't want to have to repeat myself," he said.

I heard him loud and clear. From now on, when I have a fight coming up, I wasn't supposed to have sex for two weeks. When I left the gym that day, I thought, Yeah, right. I know it's a bunch of hogwash.

But somehow, months later, I couldn't remember if I obeyed him or not.

Fourteen ⟶

THE FUTURE OF FEMALE AGGRESSION

It was a busy night. In the waiting area of the gym, the wives and girlfriends of the fighters gathered, watching over infants and children. On crowded nights, with families gathered and children playing underfoot, the place seems more like a raucous family get-together than a gym. The room was tinny with sound and activity, children screaming against a backdrop of ongoing talk, yelling, boasting, and the *rat-a-tat-tat* of the speed bag.

The three girls entered the gym in a group, giggling nervously. They looked like mall rats: fourteen to sixteen years old, in stonewashed denim jeans, tiny tennis shoes with colorful shoelaces, and teased, groomed hair. They had mascaraed eyes, cheap foundation over speckled teenage skin, carefully applied stripes of copper rouge. They inched across the floor of the gym in their tight-knit little group, as if each was an appendage of the other.

All the young boys of the gym froze, instantly alert. Unlike the few other women of the gym, who, like myself, were mostly older, these were girls like the ones at their schools: their peers—As in *girls*. The invasion was shocking and complete. Hormones, alerted, surged.

From where I was working at the heavy bag, I, too, watched the girls with interest. They were now standing, in that same little cluster, talking to Jess.

When the bell rang, signaling a break, Jess waved me over. Quick introductions were made. I immediately forgot their names, except for one—Lisa. She was the obvious leader of the group, a small young woman with long, silky blond hair, with the kind of waves you get by braiding it, and wide cornflower blue eyes, made to look even larger with a thick rim of eyeliner. She stared directly into my face.

Jess took the opportunity to vanish. I knew he didn't mean ill. For Jess, these three young girls were foreign. Boys at their age he would understand. They would be given a series of orders, expected to follow them, and would be criticized if they did it wrong and praised if they did it right. But these girls, with their giggles and feminine paraphernalia, left him lost. Besides, most of the boys who come in are brought by someone else—an older brother who trains, a father who once fought. These girls came in alone, without anyone to introduce them, show them the ropes (so to speak), chaperone their progress, and make them feel at home.

I began telling the girls about training, figuring I would fill in their unasked questions: what supplies they need to buy (hand wraps and mouthpiece), what they can expect from their coach, what kind of clothes to wear. The three of them stood in such a way as to suggest aggressiveness, with legs slightly spread, arms held away from rib cages. One, with a cap of straight brown hair, snapped her gum. The other was only half-paying attention, looking at me out of the corner of her eye.

Lisa, however, listened intently. She nodded impatiently as I droned on. Her eyes scanned my face, then flitted around the gym, cataloging the men at work on the bags, a coach watching a young boy hitting the double-end bag.

Her eyes stopped at the ring. Two boxers were sparring. The sounds of the blows—loud slapping noises—carried over to us.

Lisa assessed this for a moment, then turned back to me. Her face was demanding. "Sure," she said, clearly finding all I have said quite superfluous. "But when do I get to hit someone?"

In February of 1995, I found myself competing at a Golden Gloves tournament. It was the first time women ever competed in this tournament, which is held in Tacoma, Washington.

One of the largest on the West Coast, the Tacoma Golden Gloves tournament is organized by Tom Mustin, a renowned trainer who coached the 1995 Pan-American games. Mustin is a large black man who wears aviator-style glasses and carries himself with the dignity of a military general. He's made the Tacoma Boxing Club fighters some of the best in the nation.

The tournament was held in a college auditorium before a crowd of several thousand. The local TV news was there, as well as a crew shooting a pilot sports program for ESPN.

The skill level of the men and boys competing, many of whom had trained and competed for a lifetime, was years above that of my opponent and myself. We fought our hearts out, though.

My opponent was left-handed, a southpaw, a woman who, I found out later, works as an aerobics instructor. Her name was Sandra. She was slightly heavier than I and had Asiatic eyes. We avoided each other before the fight, barely exchanging hellos. There is something too uncomfortable about being friendly to your opponent before a fight. Not because you need to build anger—I had none—but there is just too much anxiety.

Adrenaline sucked the continuity of the fight itself out of my mind, leaving me with overexposed snapshots of memories. I remember climbing through the ropes, the sudden sense of the lights dimming, the referee signaling us to touch gloves. I remember looking into her face, and then the bell ringing. For the rest of the bout, my eyes never left hers. The fight itself was bizarre, with the crowd yelling, the lights, the metallic taste of anxiety.

I'd had other fights, but this was the first time I began to understand my own boxing as a style, rather than just a crude effort. A style Jess teaches: Go in crouched, throw lots of hooks, never relent. Always keep the pressure on.

But here I was dealing with a left-hander, which changes everything. I knew I should be throwing the right hand more, since southpaws are vulnerable to the right, and following with the left hook. When the bell rang after the first round, I went back to my corner nearly sick with nerves. Jess rinsed my mouth and caustically told me that I "looked better in the gym."

His words had the intended effect: I felt hurt and wounded. The bell rang, and I was off the stool and into the fight, desperate not to fail.

I came out swinging. I can barely remember exactly what punches I threw, the order of the combinations. Now they come at me in disjointed order, bits of confetti hailing down. I do remember one moment when she was backed toward the ropes, her head tilting back from a jab, and my left glove was swinging up to make contact in a hard hook to the side of her chin. Her head went reeling and the crowd made the sound reserved only for a good punch.

This time when I went back to my corner, Jess was pleased. He told me to win the next round, and then he pressed his hand comfortingly on my chest.

When the third bell rang, I was already off my stool, shifting my feet. All I really remember is moving forward. When

164

I felt like I was tiring, finally, toward the end of the fight— what a blur it was already—I told myself, This is it; keep going. And then I was extending those fists again, punching madly, hitting in final frustration and fear of loss.

Back in my corner, Jess told me to smile, to look good, like I'd won the fight. He unlaced the gloves and took off my helmet, and then I was led into the middle of the ring for the decision. I could only stare at the canvas, filled with dread, as the referee firmly gripped my wrist, his other hand around the wrist of my opponent.

The announcer, holding the little slips of paper from the judges, began opening his mouth to announce the decision. I heard the echoing-chamber sound of the microphone booming over the crowd before everything began going blank from nerves. And then my hand was being raised, and as I became aware of the sensation of my arm moving up, a wild, exultant excitement broke over my body. My rib cage lifted with joy. I don't think I have ever felt such pleasure, so that a picture of me at the moment would show this unrestrained, completely jubilant smile. I had won the Golden Gloves. I had never won anything important before.

A nylon Golden Gloves jacket, the classic trophy for the event, was pressed into my arms, and I cradled it, soft and chemical-smelling, back to my corner.

For a kid, the Golden Gloves would be a pinnacle. It felt a bit silly, to be twenty-seven and experiencing such pleasure in an event designed primarily for young men. But for Jess and Chuck, the delight seemed genuine. Earlier, Chuck had shown me his name under the tournament listings of past champions. Chuck Lincoln, a Golden Glove champion back in 1952. Now my name, the first female name, would enter those records.

Back where we had been sitting—with Ernesto and Anthony, who had driven up from Portland with their wives to watch the fights—Jess beamed with pride as he cut the blood-smeared tape from my hands, accepting congratulations from other coaches and fighters. My boyfriend was there, as well. It was the first time I had let him see me fight. I'd been too nervous about it before. His eyes were bright with relief.

Strangely enough, afterward it was not the fight itself that I remembered best, or even the pleasure of winning. It was something that happened right before I entered the ring. Jess and Chuck and I had left Portland at four in the morning, driving north for an early-morning weigh-in. We spent a tiring day waiting. Tom Mustin was kind enough to let us doze in his fighters' hotel room, a cheap motor inn suite with a clanking radiator and the smell of mildew. We ate in a hole-in-the-wall Chinese restaurant where the food smelled suspect.

By the time the fights started I was feeling drained. I changed into my uniform—black satin trunks made by Anthony's wife, and a black T-shirt over my chest guard, tucked into the wide band of my trunks. The team color: black. I left the locker room to warm up in a hallway, rolling my neck, shadowboxing, while cameras bathed me in white light. Jess was tense, snapping. Then my mouthpiece was being tucked in, my helmet smacked to judge snugness, and I was being trotted toward the ring, the announcer calling the bout. Time to fight.

It was then that I noticed the girl in the throng of people watching. She couldn't have been more than ten, maybe eleven. She was small and had a white face. She was with a man, maybe her father, or an older brother. Both were standing there at the front of the crowd. Her body was rigid with excitement, her face expectant.

He was leaning over her, whispering in her ear, saying, obviously, "*look.*"

I hesitate to tell this story, lest people think I believe a girl requires an older man to initiate her into aggression. But

166

isn't that what I have learned from Jess! I know now the gift he gave me transcends just boxing, this particular arena of aggression: a world within a world.

I am sure the girl would have figured it out by herself, sooner or later.

A few months later, I was told to show up earlier than my usual time, to run an offense/defense drill with a new fighter. This is when you get in the ring with someone and don't hit them but let them hit you. It's a good way to learn defense skills and introduce a beginning fighter to the ring.

I showed up and was introduced to the new fighter, a twelve-year-old girl. Under five feet and weighing maybe 105 pounds, she had silky jet black hair and huge eyes. We got ready and climbed in the ring.

At first filled with trepidation, she quickly got the hang of it; she chased me around the ring, throwing punches while I ducked, moved side to side, and caught blows on my gloves. Her eyes under her helmet were fierce, her face round and soft.

She comes in with her father and brothers, all actual and aspiring fighters. Her brothers range from eight to eighteen, and all have the same reserved manner as their father. They enter the gym in a crowd, five, six at least, of whom she is simply one more—one more set of legs warming up, one more body in a row practicing jabs across the wide wooden floor. Her dad watches over her as he does his sons, giving her advice that sounds no more critical or protective.

It was obvious to me from the first time I saw her that her affinity would not be to the other women in the gym, but to her brothers. It was to them she immediately turned between rounds, her helmet lowered through the ropes for advice. It was lovingly cuffed.

Among the families in the waiting area, the lines dividing gender no longer seem as evenly drawn as they once did.

It is here that I find evidence of a different kind of young woman: an evolution from my mother's day to mine, and beyond. From Lisa and her friends to the twelve-year-old girl, these young women seem comfortable with the idea of aggressive action.

Unlike the older women of the gym, they don't remember when women didn't compete with men. And unlike women of my age, who grew up in tumultuous times when social and legal change clashed with old views, the messages they hear aren't as contradictory, aren't as imbued with insecurity. They seem fierce, unafraid of wrangling with the boys. They have an indefinable foundation, a core belief in their abilities, which is deeply appealing in its artlessness. They don't care what I think. I'm already a relic, a dinosaur, and can offer them nothing.

As I left the gym one night, with dusk falling, the father of the twelve-year-old girl glanced up at me, fixing me with a sharp stare. I paused for a second, halfway around the corner by the door, confused.

His daughter was now in the front of the room. The neon half-light of dusk poured in through the plate-glass window, capturing everything in a soft chalk-colored air. Dressed in long, baggy trunks and an oversize shirt, her hair carefully combed off her face into a thick braid, she was shadowboxing across the floor.

She seemed as solidly rooted as if born there, a natural extension of the floor, snapping punches through the milky air. Not a phantasm or a passing fad or evocative of another era, but something as endless as history, a person of substance you can trace—like pictures of old warriors—through time. If I turned that corner today, I would expect to see her there: shadowboxing with silver feet, her blows sturdy attacks on the air, delivering devastating punches to imaginary enemies.

A woman. A fighter.

168

NOTES

One
THE FIRST DAY IN THE GYM

1. Kathleen M. Blee, *Women of the Klan: Racism and Gender in the 1920s* (Berkeley: University of California Press, 1991), 2.
2. For more on Shannon, see Spencer Heinz, "Praying with Fire: The Genesis of Shelley Shannon," *Oregonian*, November 14, 1993, among other reports. For Thompson, see Adam Parfrey and Jim Redden, "Patriot Games," *The Village Voice*, October 11, 1994.
3. Eileen MacDonald, *Shoot the Women First* (New York: Random House, 1991), 197.
4. Patrick McDowell, "Rwanda Accuses Women of Genocide," *Oregonian*, September 26, 1995. Just how many women (and men) took part in the genocide is unknown. According to the London-based organization Africa Rights, traditional views of women being peace-loving may have helped female killers escape scrutiny. Quite a few prominent Hutu women were accused of genocide, including the former prime minister of family and women's affairs, who was alleged to have joined her grown sons in nightly massacres.

Two
THE SWEET SCIENCE

1. For example, see Ira A. McCown, "Boxing Safety and Injuries," *The Physician and Sports Medicine*, 7 (March 1979): 75–82. McCown stated: "No clinical or laboratory evidence was found to substantiate the so-called punch-drunk syn-

drome that has so long been identified with boxers." For another point of view, see Ira R. Casson, et al., "Brain Damage in Modern Boxers," *Journal of the American Medical Association* 251 (May 25, 1984): 2663–2667.
2. Daniel Goleman, "A Soccer Study Links Injuries to Head Impacts," *New York Times*, August 14, 1995.
3. Tom Friend, "Heart-Rending Vigil After a Tragedy," *New York Times*, May 19, 1995.

Three
ARE WOMEN THE WEAKER SEX?

1. Phillip Anderson Bishop, "Biological Determinants of the Sex Difference in Muscular Strength" (Ed. D. dissertation: University of Georgia, 1983), 2.
2. Jacqueline L. Puhl, "Women and Endurance: Some Factors Influencing Performance," in *Female Endurance Athletes*, ed. Barbara L. Drinkwater. (Champaign, Illinois: Human Kinetics Publishers, Inc., 1986).
3. Robin Estrin, "Tests Show Women Can Pull Their Weight," *Oregonian*, January 30, 1996.
4. Bishop, "Biological Determinants of the Sex Difference in Muscular Strength," 43–45.
5. Natalie Angier, "Does Testosterone Equal Aggression? Maybe Not," *New York Times*, June 20, 1995; Natalie Angier, "Deaf to Estrogen's Call: A Man's Strange Story," *New York Times*, October 25, 1994; and Beryl Lieff Benderly, "The Testosterone Excuse," *Glamour*, March 1994, 184–258.
6. Jane E. Brody, "Aggressiveness and Delinquency in Boys Linked to Lead in Bones," *New York Times*, February 7, 1996.
7. From 7 percent, according to Ridley's 1983 source, to 13.8 percent in 1992. See Kathleen Maguire and Ann L. Pastore, eds., *Sourcebook of Criminal Justice Statistics, 1993*, U.S. Department of Justice, Bureau of Justice Statistics (Washington, D.C.: U.S. Government Printing Office, 1994), 430.
8. "Female Drivers in Fatal Crashes: Recent Trends," U.S. Department of Transportation, National Highway Traffic Safety Administration (Springfield, Virginia: National Technical Information Service, January 1994), 14. At the time of this report, women accounted for about a third of "total travel" driving.
9. Alix Kirsta, *Deadlier Than the Male: Violence and Aggression in Women* (London: HarperCollins Publishers, 1994), 47–48. The electroshocks were not real; subjects were actors and pretended to feel pain. This experiment has been replicated, with similar results.

Four
WOMEN IN ANGER: THE STEREOTYPES PROVE FALSE

1. Carol Tavris, *Anger: The Misunderstood Emotion* (New York: Touchstone, 1982), 120–150, especially 134.

Five
THE MYTH OF THE MATERNAL INSTINCT: THE UNDEREXAMINED PROBLEM OF CHILD ABUSE COMMITTED BY WOMEN

1. For example, see "Child Abuse and Neglect Report, 1994" (Salem, Oregon: Children's Services Division, Oregon Department of Human Resources, 1994). Other states show roughly the same breakdown by gender.
2. "Child Maltreatment 1993: Reports from the States to the National Center on Child Abuse and Neglect," U.S. Department of Health and Human Services, National Center on Child Abuse and Neglect (Washington, D.C: U.S. Government Printing Office, 1995), 2–2.
3. Ibid., 2–6.
4. Kathleen Maguire and Ann L. Pastore, eds., *Sourcebook of Criminal Justice Statistics, 1993*, U.S. Department of Justice, Bureau of Justice Statistics (Washington, D.C.: U.S. Government Printing Office, 1994), 278.
5. For example, see David Finkelhor, *Child Sexual Abuse* (New York: The Free Press, 1984), 171–185.
6. Ruth Mathews, Jane Kinder Matthews, and Kathleen Speltz, *Female Sexual Offenders: An Exploratory Study* (Orwell, Vermont: The Safer Society Press, 1989).

Six
VIOLENCE IN RELATIONSHIPS: IT'S NOT ALWAYS A ONE-WAY STREET

1. Information about these surveys has been taken from Murray A. Straus, Richard J. Gelles, and Suzanne K. Steinmetz, *Behind Closed Doors: Violence in the American Family* (New York: Anchor Books, 1980), Richard J. Gelles and Murray A. Straus, *Intimate Violence: The Causes and Consequences of Abuse in the American Family* (New York: Touchstone, 1988), and Murray A. Straus, Glenda Kaufman Kantor, and David W. Moore, "Change in Cultural Norms Approving Marital Violence," paper presented at the annual meeting of the American Sociological Association, Los Angeles, August 7, 1994, and Murray A. Straus and Glenda Kaufman Kantor, "Change in Assault Rates From 1975 to 1992: A Comparison of Three National Surveys in the United States," paper presented at the 13th World Congress of Sociology, Bielefeld, Germany, July 19, 1994.
2. For an overview, see Murray A. Straus, "Physical Assaults by Wives: A Major Social Problem," in *Current Controversies on Family Violence*, eds. Richard J. Gelles and Donileen R. Loseke (Newbury Park, California: Sage Publications, 1993), 69–70. For examples of studies, see Lisa D. Brush, "Violent Acts and Injurious Outcomes in Married Couples: Methodological Issues in the National Survey of Families and Households," *Gender and Society* 4 (March 1990): 56–67,

and Wendy G. Goldberg and Michael C. Tomlanovich, "Domestic Violence Victims in the Emergency Department," *Journal of the American Medical Association* 251 (June 1984): 3259–3264.

3. For example, see Gwat-Yong Lie and Sabrina Gentlewarrier, "Intimate Violence in Lesbian Relationships: Discussion of Survey Findings and Practice Implications," *Journal of Social Service Research* 15 (1991): 41–59, and Rebecca Schilit and Gwat-Yong Lie, "Substance Use as a Correlate of Violence in Intimate Lesbian Relationships," *Journal of Homosexuality* 19 (1990): 51–65.

4. Joelle Taylor and Tracey Chandler, *Lesbians Talk Violent Relationships* (London: Scarlet Press, 1995), 36.

5. Straus, "Physical Assaults by Wives," 70.

6. Straus, Gelles, and Steinmetz, *Behind Closed Doors*, 34, and Gelles and Straus, *Intimate Violence*, 275 n. 99.

7. John Griffith, "Husband Survives the Lumps and Bumps of a New Marriage," *Oregonian*, June 26, 1993.

8. Janell D. Schmidt and Lawrence W. Sherman, "Does Arrest Deter Domestic Violence?" *American Behavioral Scientist* 36 (May 1993): 601–609.

Seven
CRIMINAL WOMEN

1. Unless otherwise noted, all arrest statistics are from Kathleen Maguire and Ann L. Pastore, eds., *Sourcebook of Criminal Justice Statistics, 1993*, U.S. Department of Justice, Bureau of Justice Statistics (Washington, D.C.: United States Government Printing Office, 1994), 430.

2. John M. Dawson and Patrick A. Langan, "Murder in Families," Bureau of Justice Statistics Special Report (Washington, D.C.: U.S. Department of Justice, July 1994), 1.

3. Raymond Hernandez, "Mother Gets 75 Years for Smothering 5 of Her Children," *New York Times*, September 12, 1995.

4. Estimates of female-perpetrated homicide vary from 10 percent to 16 percent. I am using a 14 percent figure, calculated from 1989 Federal Bureau of Investigation statistics by social scientist Murray Straus. See Straus, "Physical Assaults by Wives: A Major Social Problem," in *Current Controversies on Family Violence*, eds. Richard J. Gelles and Donileen R. Loseke (Newbury Park, California: Sage Publications, 1993), 72.

5. Dawson and Langan, "Murder in Families," 3.

6. S. Fernando Rodriguez and Veronica A. Henderson, "Intimate Homicide: Victim-Offender Relationship in Female-Perpetrated Homicide," *Deviant Behavior: An Interdisciplinary Journal* 16 (1995): 50.

7. Dawson and Langan, "Murder in Families," 5. See also Susan Chira, "Murdered Children: In Most Cases, a Parent Did It," *New York Times*, November 5, 1994.

8. Matthew Scanlon, "Women in Prison," *Psychology Today*, November/December 1993, 45.

9. Lawrence A. Greenfeld and James J. Stephen, "Capital Punishment 1992," Bureau of Justice Bulletin (Washington, D.C.: U.S. Department of Justice,

December 1993), 7, and Don Terry, "After a Life of Desperation, A Female Inmate Asks to Die," *New York Times*, January 8, 1996.

10. For more on gender bias in the justice system, see Ilene H. Nagel and Barry L. Johnson, "The Role of Gender in a Structured Sentencing System: Equal Treatment, Policy Choices, and the Sentencing of Female Offenders Under the United States Sentencing Guidelines," *Journal of Criminal Law and Criminology* 85 (1994): 181–221, and Darrell J. Steffensmeier and Emilie Andersen Allan, "Sex Disparities in Arrests by Residence, Race, and Age: An Assessment of the Gender Convergence/Crime Hypothesis," *Justice Quarterly* 5 (March 1988): 53–80. These authors also point out socialized gender differences during the high crime years.

11. John M. Dawson and Barbara Boland, "Murder in Large Urban Counties, 1988," Bureau of Justice Statistics Special Report (Washington, D.C.: U.S. Department of Justice, May 1993), 9, table 15.

12. Alan M. Dershowitz, "Wives Also Kill Husbands—Quite Often," *Los Angeles Times*, July 21, 1994.

13. Nagel and Johnson, "The Role of Gender in a Structured Sentencing System," 188–189.

14. Coramae Richey Mann, "Getting Even? Women Who Kill in Domestic Encounters," *Justice Quarterly* 5 (March 1988), 48.

15. Joyce Wadler and Lorenzo Benet, "Rage of a Woman Scorned," *People*, October 21, 1991, 68.

16. Frances M. Heidensohn, *Women and Crime: The Life of the Female Offender*, (New York: New York University Press, 1985), 155.

17. Allison Morris, *Women, Crime and Criminal Justice* (New York: Basil Blackwell, 1987) 70–71.

18. Margo I. Wilson and Martin Daly, "Who Kills Whom in Spouse Killings? On the Exceptional Sex Ratio of Spousal Homicides in the United States," *Criminology* 30 (1992), 196.

Eight
THE POWER OF FEAR

1. Mark Warr, "Public Perceptions and Reactions to Violent Offending and Victimization," in *Understanding and Preventing Violence*, vol. 4, eds. Albert J. Reiss, Jr. and Jeffrey A. Roth (Washington, D.C.: National Academy Press, 1994), 12.

2. "Big Increase Found for Assaults and Robberies," *New York Times*, October 31, 1994.

3. Randy L. LaGrange and Kenneth F. Ferraro, "Assessing Age and Gender Differences in Perceived Risk and Fear of Crime," *Criminology* 27 (1989): 697–719. About one in ten men feared sexual assault, compared with one in two women.

4. Warr, "Public Perceptions and Reactions to Violent Offending and Victimization," 24.

5. Katherine Dunn, "Crime and Embellishment," *Los Angeles Times Magazine*, April 10, 1994.

6. Tina Rosenberg, "The Deadliest D.A.," *New York Times Magazine*, July 16, 1995, 23.

7. Lisa D. Bastian, "Criminal Victimization in the United States: 1973–90 Trends," Bureau of Justice Statistics (Washington, D.C.: U.S. Department of Justice, December 1992).

8. W. Fitzhugh Brundage, *Lynching in the New South: Georgia and Virginia, 1880–1930*, (Urbana: University of Illinois Press, 1993), 37–42, and 259.

9. Kathleen Blee, *Women of the Klan: Racism and Gender in the 1920s* (Berkeley: University of California Press, 1991), 1–3, 123–153. Also see Wyn Craig Wade, *The Fiery Cross: The Ku Klux Klan in America* (New York: Touchstone, 1987), 225 and 230.

Nine
JESS

1. "Holmes Concedes He's Getting Hit," *New York Times*, September 21, 1995.

Ten
WOMEN IN THE MILITARY

1. "Success Rates for Combat Arms Occupational Qualification Training, 1994–1995," from the offices of the Canadian National Defense Headquarters, courtesy of Chris Lemay.

2. Michael E. Ruane, "Women Soldiers: Striding to the Front Line," *Oregonian*, October 26, 1994.

3. "Sailing into Motherhood," *New York Times*, February 11, 1995.

4. Kate Muir, *Arms and the Woman* (London: Sinclair-Stevenson, 1992), 18–19.

5. Amy Pagnozzi, "The Real Reason Men Want to Keep Women Soldiers Out of Combat," *Glamour*, December 1992.

6. Paul Pinkham and Susan P. Respess, "Sailor Gets 30 Months for Sodomy," *Florida Times-Union*, May 20, 1993, and Paul Pinkham, "Navy Man Convicted of Rape," *Florida Times-Union*, May 21, 1993.

7. Sara Rimer, "Women 'Are No Big Deal' at an Old Military College," *New York Times*, September 6, 1995.

8. Tim Weiner, "Sexual Harassment in Military Dips, but Remains Problem, Survey Finds," *New York Times*, July 3, 1996.

9. "Women in Combat," Transcript of the hearing before the Military Forces and Personnel Subcommittee of the Committee on Armed Services (Washington, D.C.: U.S. Government Printing Office, 1994), 51–52.

10. David Wood, "Black Women Get Ahead in Military," *Oregonian*, February 4, 1996.

Eleven
FEMALE COMPETITION

1. Cynthia Fuchs Epstein, "Women's Attitudes Toward Other Women—Myths and Their Consequences," *American Journal of Psychotherapy* 34 (July 1980): 326.

Twelve
WOMEN IN SPORTS

1. Salvatore Carlino, "Title IX: A Legislative History, Selected Court Cases, and the Future of Women's Athletic Programs" (master's thesis Pennsylvania State University, 1985), 19.
2. Jane Gottesman, "Is Cheerleading a Sneaky Way Around Title IX?" *New York Times*, October 23, 1994.
3. Ibid.
4. Jennifer Steinhauer, "Teen-Age Girls Talk Back on Exercise," *New York Times*, January 4, 1995.
5. Jere Longman, "As Parents Squirm, Women Happily Scrum," *New York Times*, May 8, 1995.
6. "The High Court Confronts Sex Bias," *New York Times*, January 17, 1996.

SELECTED
BIBLIOGRAPHY

Adler, Freda. *Sisters in Crime: The Rise of the New Female Criminal.* New York: McGraw-Hill, 1975.

———, ed. *The Incidence of Female Criminality in the Contemporary World.* New York: New York University Press, 1984.

Baunach, Phyllis Jo. *Mothers in Prison.* New Brunswick, New Jersey: Transaction, 1985.

Beals, Melba Pattillo. *Warriors Don't Cry: A Searing Memoir of the Battle to Integrate Little Rock's Central High.* New York: Pocket Books, 1994.

Beckerman, Adela. "Mothers in Prison: Meeting the Prerequisite Conditions for Permanency Planning." *Social Work* 39 (January 1994): 9–14.

Bentley, Judith. *Busing: The Continuing Controversy.* New York: Impact Books, 1982.

Blais, Madeleine. *In These Girls, Hope Is a Muscle: A True Story of Hoop Dreams and One Very Special Team.* New York: Warner Books, 1995.

Blee, Kathleen M. *Women of the Klan: Racism and Gender in the 1920s.* Berkeley: University of California Press, 1991.

Briggs, Freda. *From Victim to Offender: How Child Sexual Abuse Victims Become Offenders.* St. Leonards, Australia: Allen & Unwin, 1995.

Brown, C. Harmon, and Jack H. Wilmore. "The Effects of Maximal Resistance Training on the Strength and Body Composition of Women Athletes." *Medicine and Science in Sports* 6 (1974): 174–177.

Brundage, W. Fitzhugh. *Lynching in the New South: Georgia and Virginia, 1880–1930.* Urbana: University of Illinois Press, 1993.

Brush, Lisa D. "Violent Acts and Injurious Outcomes in Married Couples." *Gender & Society* 4 (March 1990): 56–67.

Buzawa, Eve S., and Carl G. Buzawa, eds. "The Impact of Arrest on Domestic Violence." Issue devoted to topic, with articles by Barbara Hart, Richard J. Gelles, Peter K. Manning, Janell D. Schmidt, Lawrence W. Sherman, Evan

Selected Bibliography

Stark, and Murray A. Straus. *American Behavioral Scientist* 36 (May/June 1993).

Campbell, Anne. *The Girls in the Gang.* Cambridge, Massachusetts: Blackwell, 1991.

————. *Men, Women, and Aggression: From Rage in Marriage to Violence in the Streets—How Gender Affects the Way We Act.* New York: Basic Books, 1993.

Casson, Ira R., et al. "Brain Damage in Modern Boxers." *Journal of the American Medical Association* 251 (May 25, 1984): 2663–2667.

"Child Abuse and Neglect Report, 1994." Salem, Oregon: Children's Services Division, Oregon Department of Human Resources, 1994.

"Child Maltreatment 1993: Reports from the States to the National Center on Child Abuse and Neglect." U.S. Department of Health and Human Services, National Center on Child Abuse and Neglect. Washington, D.C.: U.S. Government Printing Office, 1995.

Christensen, Loren. *Skinhead Street Gangs.* Boulder, Colorado: Paladin Press, 1994.

Clark, Roger. "Cross-National Perspectives on Female Crime: An Empirical Investigation." *International Journal of Comparative Sociology* 30 (September/December 1989): 195–215.

Daly, Kathleen. "Gender and Varieties of White-Collar Crime." *Criminology* 27 (1989): 769–794.

Daly, Kathleen, and Meda Chesney-Lind. "Feminism and Criminology." *Justice Quarterly* 5 (December 1988): 497–538.

Dawson, John M., and Barbara Boland. "Murder in Large Urban Counties, 1988." Bureau of Justice Statistics Special Report. Washington, D.C.: U.S. Department of Justice, May 1993.

Dawson, John M., and Patrick A. Langan. "Murder in Families." Bureau of Justice Statistics Special Report. Washington, D.C.: U.S. Department of Justice, July 1994.

Denno, Deborah W. "Gender, Crime, and the Criminal Law Defenses." *The Journal of Law and Criminology* 85 (Summer 1994): 80–165.

Dixon, Gerald Ernest. "The Study of Boxing as an Intercollegiate Sport." Master's thesis University of Wisconsin, 1972.

Dobash, Russell P., R. Emerson Dobash, Margo Wilson, and Martin Daly. "The Myth of Sexual Symmetry in Marital Violence." *Social Problems* 39 (February 1992): 71–91.

Drinkwater, Barbara L. *Female Endurance Athletes.* Champaign, Illinois: Human Kinetics Publishers, Inc., 1986.

Epstein, Cynthia Fuchs. "Women's Attitudes Toward Other Women— Myths and Their Consequences." *American Journal of Psychotherapy* 34 (July 1980): 322–333.

Fahey, Thomas D., Richard Rolph, Pratoom Moungmee, James Nagel, and Stephen Mortara. "Serum Testosterone, Body Composition, and Strength of Young Adults." *Medicine and Science in Sports* 8 (1976): 31–34.

Finkelhor, David. *Child Sexual Abuse.* New York: Free Press, 1984.

Flowers, Ronald Barri. *Women and Criminality: The Woman as Victim, Offender, and Practitioner.* Westport, Connecticut: Greenwood Press, 1987.

Friedman, Lawrence M. *Crime and Punishment in American History.* New York: Basic Books, 1993.

SELECTED BIBLIOGRAPHY

Gelles, Richard J., and Murray A. Straus. *Intimate Violence: The Causes and Consequences of Abuse in the American Family*. New York: Touchstone, 1988.

Gelles, Richard J., and Donileen R. Loseke, eds. *Current Controversies on Family Violence*. Newbury Park, California: Sage Publications, 1993.

"Gender Discrimination in the Military." Hearings before the Military Personnel and Compensation Subcommittee and the Defense Policy Panel. Washington, D.C.: U.S. Government Printing Office, 1992.

Georges-Abeyie, Daniel E. "Women as Terrorists." In *Perspectives on Terrorism*, edited by Lawrence Zelic Freedman and Yonah Alexander. Wilmington, Delaware: Scholarly Resources Inc., 1983.

Girdner, Audrie, and Anne Loftis. *The Great Betrayal: The Evacuation of the Japanese-Americans During World War II*. London: The MacMillan Company, 1969.

Goldberg, Wendy G., and Michael C. Tomlanovich. "Domestic Violence Victims in the Emergency Department." *Journal of the American Medical Association*, 251 (June 22–29, 1984): 3259–3264.

Greenfeld, Lawrence A., and James J. Stephen. "Capital Punishment 1992." Bureau of Justice Statistics Bulletin. Washington, D.C.: U.S. Department of Justice, December 1993.

Guttmann, Allen. *Women's Sports: A History*. New York: Columbia University Press, 1991.

Harvey, Linda, R. W. Burnham, Kathy Kendall, and Ken Pease. "Gender Differences in Criminal Justice." *The British Journal of Criminology* 32 (Winter 1992): 208–217.

Heidensohn, Frances M. *Women and Crime: The Life of the Female Offender*. New York: New York University Press, 1985.

Holm, Jeanne. *Women in the Military: An Unfinished Revolution*, rev. ed. Novato, California: Presidio Press, 1992.

Hornung, Carlton A., B. Claire McCullough, and Taichi Sugimoto. "Status Relationships in Marriage: Risk Factors in Spouse Abuse." *Journal of Marriage and the Family* 251 (August 1981): 675–692.

Hubbard, Ruth. *The Politics of Women's Biology*. New Brunswick, New Jersey: Rutgers University Press, 1990.

Jankowski, Louis W. "Jail Inmates 1991." Bureau of Justice Statistics Bulletin. Washington, D.C.: U.S. Department of Justice, 1991.

Jones, Ann. *Women Who Kill*. New York: Fawcett Columbine, 1981.

Kaminer, Wendy. *It's All the Rage: Crime and Culture*. New York: Addison-Wesley, 1995.

Kirsta, Alix. *Deadlier Than the Male: Violence and Aggression in Women*. London: HarperCollins, 1994.

Klama, John. *Aggression: The Myth of the Beast Within*. New York: John Wiley & Sons, 1988.

LaGrange, Randy L., and Kenneth F. Ferraro. "Assessing Age and Gender Differences in Perceived Risk and Fear of Crime." *Criminology* 27 (November 1989): 697–719.

Lambert, Pater W., and John M. Hardman. "Morphological Changes in Brains of Boxers." *Journal of the American Medical Association* 251 (May 25, 1984): 2676–2679.

Lie, Gwat-Yong, and Sabrina Gentlewarrier. "Intimate Violence in Lesbian

Selected Bibliography

Relationships: Discussion of Survey Findings and Practice Implications." *Journal of Social Science Research* 15 (1991): 41–59.

Lobel, Kerry, ed. *Naming the Violence: Speaking Out About Lesbian Battering.* Seattle: Seal Press, 1986.

Lorenz, Konrad. *On Aggression.* New York: Bantam Books, 1967.

MacDonald, Eileen. *Shoot the Women First.* New York: Random House, 1991.

Maguire, Kathleen, and Ann L. Pastore, eds. *Sourcebook of Criminal Justice Statistics, 1993.* U.S. Department of Justice, Bureau of Justice Statistics. Washington, D.C.: U.S. Government Printing Office, 1994.

Mann, Coramae Richey. "Getting Even? Women Who Kill In Domestic Encounters." *Justice Quarterly* 5 (March 1988): 33–51.

Mathews, Ruth, Jane Kinder Matthews, and Kathleen Speltz. *Female Sexual Offenders: An Exploratory Study.* Orwell, Vermont: Safer Society Press, 1989.

McCown, Ira A. "Boxing Safety and Injuries." *The Physician and Sports Medicine* 7 (March 1979): 75–82.

McNeely, R. L., and Gloria Robinson-Simpson. "The Truth About Domestic Violence: A Falsely Framed Issue." *Social Work*, November–December 1987, 485–489.

Mead, Margaret. *Male and Female: A Study of the Sexes in a Changing World.* New York: William Morrow and Company, 1975.

"Military Women in the Department of Defense," vol. 6. Washington, D.C.: U.S. Government Printing Office, July 1988.

Montagu, Ashley, ed. *Man and Aggression.* New York: Oxford University Press, 1968.

————, ed. *Learning Non-Aggression: The Experience of Non-Literate Societies.* New York: Oxford University Press, 1978.

————, *The Nature of Human Aggression.* New York: Oxford University Press, 1976.

Morris, Allison. *Women, Crime and Criminal Justice.* New York: Basil Blackwell, 1987.

Morrow, James R., Jr., and W. W. Hosler. "Strength Comparisons in Untrained Men and Trained Women Athletes." *Medicine and Science in Sports and Exercise*, 13 (1981): 194–197.

Muir, Kate. *Arms and the Woman.* London: Sinclair-Stevenson, 1992.

Nagel, Ilene H., and Barry L. Johnson. "The Role of Gender in a Structured Sentencing System: Equal Treatment, Policy Choices, and the Sentencing of Female Offenders Under the United States Sentencing Guidelines." *The Journal of Criminal Law and Criminology* 85 (Summer 1994): 181–221.

Nelson, Mariah Burton. *Are We Winning Yet? How Women Are Changing Sports and Sports Are Changing Women.* New York: Random House, 1991.

Oates, Joyce Carol. *On Boxing.* Hopewell, New Jersey: Ecco Press, 1994.

Pagelow, Mildred Daley. *Woman-Battering: Victims and Their Experiences.* Beverly Hills: Sage Publications, 1981.

Pollack, Otto. *The Criminality of Women.* New York: A. S. Barnes & Company, 1961.

Pollock-Byrne, Joycelyn M. *Women, Prison, and Crime.* Belmont, California: Wadsworth, 1990.

Rafter, Nicole Hahn. *Partial Justice: Women, Prisons, and Social Control.* New Brunswick, New Jersey: Transaction, 1995.

Renzetti, Claire M. *Violent Betrayal: Partner Abuse in Lesbian Relationships*. Newbury Park, California: Sage Publications, 1992.

"Report to the President." The Presidential Commission on the Assignment of Women in the Armed Forces. Washington, D.C.: U.S. Government Printing Office, November 15, 1992.

Ridley, Matt. *The Red Queen: Sex and the Evolution of Human Nature*. New York: Macmillan, 1993.

Rodriguez, S. Fernando, and Veronica A. Henderson. "Intimate Homicide: Victim-Offender Relationship in Female-Perpetrated Homicide." *Deviant Behavior: An Interdisciplinary Journal* 16 (January/March 1995): 45–57.

Schilit, Rebecca, and Gwat-Yong Lie. "Substance Abuse as a Correlate of Violence in Intimate Lesbian Relationships." *Journal of Homosexuality* 19 (1990): 51–65.

Schneider, Dorothy, and Carl J. Schneider. *Sound Off! American Military Women Speak Out*. New York: E. P. Dutton, 1988.

Simon, Rita J., and Jean Landis. *The Crimes Women Commit, The Punishments They Receive*. Lexington, Massachusetts: Lexington Books, 1991.

Sims, Patsy. *The Klan*. New York: Stein and Day, 1978.

Smith, Elizabeth Simpson. *Breakthrough: Women in Law Enforcement*. New York: Walker, 1982.

Snell, Tracy L. "Women in Prison: Survey of State Prison Inmates, 1991." Bureau of Justice Statistics Special Report. Washington, D.C.: U.S. Department of Justice, March 1994.

Sommers, Ira, and Deborah R. Baskin. "The Situational Context of Violent Female Offending." *Journal of Research in Crime and Delinquency* 30 (May 1993): 136–162.

Steffensmeier, Darrell J., and Emilie Andersen Allan. "Sex Disparities in Arrests By Residence, Race, and Age: An Assessment of the Gender Convergence/Crime Hypothesis." *Justice Quarterly* 5 (March 1988): 53–80.

Steinmetz, Suzanne K. "Women and Violence: Victims and Perpetrators." *American Journal of Psychotherapy* 34 (July 1980): 334–350.

Straus, Murray A., Richard J. Gelles, and Suzanne K. Steinmetz. *Behind Closed Doors: Violence in the American Family*. New York: Anchor Books, 1980.

Straus, Murray A., and Glenda Kaufman Kantor. "Change in Spouse Assault Rates from 1975 to 1992: A Comparison of Three National Surveys in the United States." Paper presented at the 13th World Congress of Sociology, Bielefeld, Germany, July 19, 1994.

———, David W. Moore, "Change in Cultural Norms Approving Marital Violence From 1968 to 1994." Paper presented at the annual meeting of the American Sociological Association, Los Angeles, California, August 7, 1994.

Tavris, Carol. *Anger: The Misunderstood Emotion*. New York: Touchstone, 1982.

Taylor, Joelle, and Tracey Chandler. *Lesbians Talk Violent Relationships*. London: Scarlet Press, 1995.

Tracy, Laura. *The Secret Between Us: Competition Among Women*. Boston: Little, Brown, 1991.

Valentis, Mary, and Anne Devane. *Female Rage: Unlocking Its Secrets, Claiming Its Power*. New York: Clarkson Potter, 1994.

181

Selected Bibliography

Van Hasselt, Vincent B., Randall L. Morrison, Alan S. Bellack, and Michel Hersen, eds. *Handbook of Family Violence.* New York: Plenum Press, 1988.

Vetter, Harold J., and Gary R. Perlstein. *Perspectives on Terrorism.* Pacific Grove, California: Brooks/Cole Publishing Company, 1991.

Wade, Wyn Craig. *The Fiery Cross: The Ku Klux Klan in America.* New York: Touchstone, 1987.

Walker, Lenore E. *The Battered Woman Syndrome.* New York: Springer Publishing Company, 1984.

———. *Terrifying Love: Why Battered Women Kill and How Society Responds.* New York: Harper & Row, 1989.

Warr, Mark. "Fear of Victimization: Why Are Women and the Elderly More Afraid?" *Social Science Quarterly* 65 (September 1984): 681–702.

———. "Fear of Rape Among Urban Women." *Social Problems* 32 (February 1985): 238–248.

———. "What Is the Perceived Seriousness of Crimes?" *Criminology* 27 (1989): 795–821.

———. "Public Perceptions and Reactions to Violent Offending and Victimization." In *Understanding and Preventing Violence*, vol. 4, edited by Albert J. Reiss, Jr., and Jeffrey A. Roth. Washington, D.C.: National Academy Press, 1994.

White, Jacquelyn W., and Robin M. Kowalski. "Deconstructing the Myth of the Nonaggressive Woman." *Psychology of Women Quarterly* 18 (December 1994): 487–508.

Williams, Christine L. *Gender Differences at Work: Women and Men in Nontraditional Occupations.* Berkeley and Los Angeles: University of California Press, 1989.

Wilmore, Jack H. "Alterations in Strength, Body Composition and Anthropometric Measurements Consequent to a 10-Week Weight Training Program." *Medicine and Science in Sports* 6 (1974): 133–138.

Wilson, Margo I., and Martin Daly. "Who Kills Whom in Spouse Killings? On the Exceptional Sex Ratio of Spousal Homicide in the United States." *Criminology* 30 (May 1992): 189–216.

"Women in the Army Policy Review." Office of the Deputy Chief of Staff for Personnel, Department of the Army. Washington, D.C.: U.S. Government Printing Office, November 1982.

"Women in Combat." Hearing before the Military Forces and Personnel Subcommittee of the Committee on Armed Services. Washington, D.C.: U.S. Government Printing Office, 1994.

Wright, Robert. *The Moral Animal: Why We Are the Way We Are: The New Science of Evolutionary Psychology.* New York: Pantheon Books, 1994.

Zimmerman, Jean. *Tailspin: Women at War in the Wake of Tailhook.* New York: Doubleday, 1995.